The Gig Economy

The Economy | Key Ideas

These short primers introduce students to the core concepts, theories and models, both new and established, heterodox and mainstream, contested and accepted, used by economists and political economists to understand and explain the workings of the economy.

Published

Behavioural Economics
Graham Mallard

Degrowth
Giorgos Kallis

The Gig Economy
Alex De Ruyter and Martyn Brown

The Informal Economy
Colin C. Williams

The Living Wage
Donald Hirsch and Laura Valadez-Martinez

Marginalism
Bert Mosselmans

The Resource Curse
S. Mansoob Murshed

The Gig Economy

Alex De Ruyter and Martyn Brown

agenda
publishing

First published in 2019 by Agenda Publishing

Agenda Publishing Limited
The Core
Bath Lane
Newcastle Helix
Newcastle upon Tyne
NE4 5TF
www.agendapub.com

ISBN 978-1-78821-004-1 (hardcover)
ISBN 978-1-78821-005-8 (paperback)

British Library Cataloguing-in-Publication Data
A catalogue record for this book is available from the British Library

Typeset by JS Typesetting Ltd, Porthcawl, Mid Glamorgan
Printed and bound in the UK by TJ International

Contents

1

Introduction

The purpose of this book is to explain in a concise manner to a non-specialist readership what is meant by the "gig economy", how it operates and what implications it poses for the workers and businesses that operate within its confines, and what issues it raises for the wider economy and society. In seeking to assess this phenomenon, this book above all adopts a historical perspective.

A key posit is that the gig economy is just the latest trend catchphrase capturing a spectrum of flexible (or precarious) work arrangements that have existed in one form or another since the ascendancy of capitalism in the sixteenth century. Indeed, it could be argued that such work arrangements, aside from the post-Second World War welfare state phase in mature, western states, have constituted the dominant arrangement in capitalist societies. The gig economy then could be interpreted as "old wine in a new bottle". However, the emergence of the gig economy has also been posited in terms of technological advancements that have led to the automation of certain functions and the coming together of information technology and telecommunications technologies.

This has led to the superseding of traditional firm structures, in the sense that the "transaction costs" identified by Ronald Coase in 1937 (Coase 1937) associated with contracting on the open market have been reduced by such technological change and hence lessened the perceived need for employment (as opposed to market) relationships by such firms. As such, there is a clear need to get behind the label of gig economy and gain an understanding of the objective conditions of work surrounding such jobs, gain an understanding of the motives and business models of companies that seek to utilize workers under such arrangements, and hence identify the factors that have driven growth of such jobs. In the next section, we begin by exploring the origins of the term "gig" and thereby seek to understand the evolution of its discourse to now being used to describe a key structural feature of modern capitalist economies.

Introduction

The word "gig" is used to denote many things, often bearing little relation to one another, still less to any "original" meaning. Yet this very diversity may give us some indication of what this phenomenon means in terms of the economy. Jack Barsky, a KGB spy operating in the US who upon being caught in 2010, recalled "I knew the gig was up" (Barsky & Coloma 2017). One of the current authors was invited to take the role of external examiner for a university in Greece, which the previous incumbent described as "a good gig". Similarly, a senior manager, academic and government advisor from a major UK university referred to a recent trip to Romania, where he was delivering a speech to government ministers as an "interesting gig". The word "gig" is versatile to say the least. The gig economy also seems to have reached the status of stock phrase and rarely does a day pass when the media fails to run a story on it, so that it has now become as integral to our lives as Brexit.

Given the import and currency of the gig economy there is surprisingly little written on the subject by academics. Yet there is a clear need for published work to document, conceptualize and contextualize these developments to facilitate a move beyond the narrow focus on "employment" to embrace a wider critical debate on the utility and meaning of "work". Perhaps the lack of interest in the phenomenon is symptomatic of the "taken for granted" nature of the phrase and the word. But the word "gig", it will be argued, is in many ways well suited to describe the phenomenon. This chapter does not seek definitions in the time-honoured way, but the inexact connotations and nuanced meanings will help us understand why the word "gig" has been allied more recently to the word "economy" and to what effect.

The nature of gig work

One of the earliest uses of the word "gig" was in the medieval period where a gig referred to something that spins around. Indeed, the rotary washing line, a relatively recent invention, is sometimes colloquially referred to as a "whirligig".[1] The only stable pattern the whirligig has is its rotatory motion, but the direction, speed and frequency of rotation is unpredictable, sporadic and temporary, subject to the vicissitudes of the wind. These days however, a gig is most commonly associated with the entertainments industry, and it is to this world we turn for our most helpful insights into the gig economy.

In the entertainments industry, a gig is a public performance, often a one-off event yet sometimes repeated or even regular, usually paid, but maybe not. The gig might be the result of careful marketing or simply fortuitous, but is more likely to be unpredictable and precarious.

A key feature of the life of a working musician is the notion of the "dep"; an abbreviation of the word "deputy" or "deputization". Unlike gig work in the context of the gig economy, a dep in the music business is someone often very skilled at reading music and/or extremely versatile in terms of performance styles and who is hired to stand in for another musician, whose gig it was, because the latter cannot make it for some reason. The dep can be seen as similar to the notion of the freelancer (which originally appeared in the novel *Ivanhoe* by Sir Walter Scott and refers to Italian and French mercenaries willing to offer their ability with a lance in return for payment from the nobility wishing to protect their land): a band might actually consist of a number of deps, occasionally there are more deps than regular members. Smart band leaders develop and maintain a list of reliable deps continuously and a full band is, for many such leaders, never more than a few phone calls away.

While some musicians are seen as regular deps, the one-night stand is a more common feature of the life of a working musician. The one-night stand has of course, another connotation, a one-off amorous encounter, but in this instance the phrase is used to distinguish the single night of paid work from more stable (yet still notoriously unstable) work, sometimes referred to as a "residency". This meant more to musicians 30–40 years ago than it does today. A resident gig would typically be one in which a band leader would hire musicians to fulfil a contract he or she has with a particular venue. Musicians are hired mainly for their ability to play the written music in front of them, often without rehearsal, but reliability is a key factor too. Band leaders frequently move from being simply leaders of bands to being quasi

---

1. See https://en.wikipedia.org/wiki/Whirligig (accessed 15 October 2018).

agents hiring and paying the musicians and taking a cut from the overall fee as well as their own fee for playing and leading.

Resident gigs were usually coveted because they provided a relatively stable source of income, albeit again temporarily, allowing the musician to play more satisfying music elsewhere that didn't pay as well or at all. The Musicians' Union (MU) in the UK insisted that musicians be paid a minimum amount but this only prevailed in certain formal settings, such as theatres, shows, television and radio work as well as professional orchestras and cruise liners engaging musicians for contracts lasting months and travelling the world. The MU was then largely the preserve of professional musicians and its pronouncements largely bypassed informal social club bands and summer seasons at holiday camps. By most accounts even though this kind of work could be repetitive and boring, it could, in turn, be cash-in-hand and so bypass the taxman.

At the beginning of the twentieth century the word "gig" was associated with American jazz musicians who would refer to an engagement as a gig. There is also the enchanting possibility that the word gig was originally an acronym for "God is Good", a phrase used by those musicians in thanks for having been offered paid work.[2] "God is Good" conveys the fortuitous nature of the paid work and potential divine intervention. Whether this is true or not, the notion offers some help in understanding the phenomenon; namely that people offered a gig may be in some way grateful to someone else, and it also suggests that they are unable to make that happen for themselves, relying instead on the good graces of others to provide them with work and therefore income, either way, gigs were temporary, infrequent and badly paid.

The nature of the gig worker and the gig relationship

Now, in the twenty-first century, the word "gig" has come to mean any performance, task or engagement at all, paid or otherwise, regular or not. Indeed, the word is no longer even used to refer to live music and is routinely used by musicians, DJs and indeed audiences all over the world. The nature of gig work has been characterized here as temporary, unreliable and

---

2. See https://www.allacronyms.com/GIG/God_is_good (accessed 16 October 2018).

fortuitous, but what about the characteristics of the gig worker? Perhaps the most abiding impression created by the notion of the gig economy is that of the gig worker as a free agent pursuing the next job in return for money, yet in no way beholden to the company that supplies the work: free to pursue whatever he or she wishes and even not to work at all if they so choose, with no semblance of any long-term expectations attached to any work that they undertake.

What about the relationship between the gig worker and the "employer"? We would not be the first to have noted the pre-existence of the gig economy. Harvey *et al.* (2017) have argued that the advent of the current gig economy is well described as a form of "neo-villeiny". Villeiny was a feudal arrangement of the Middle Ages in which the worker was in bondage to the lord to whom was paid a rent for the right to work the land even though there was no guaranteed income from the land in terms of crops. Labour was speculative and unpaid, and benefited the landowner.

But is it substantially different now? In their survey of UK self-employed personal trainers working from fitness centres they found the same conditions exist in the twenty-first century; an expansion of hyper-flexible and precarious work. The authors note however that many of the personal trainers they surveyed through participant observation had "chosen" this arrangement as a route to independent income and a way to embrace entrepreneurialism. However, Harvey *et al.* also revealed that the personal trainers working in this way pay the fitness centre rent and have no guarantee of income while doing unpaid and speculative work that benefits the organization (*ibid.*).

Tempting as it is to argue that we have returned to a feudal economy (but with a more palatable name), the current notion of the gig economy, some have argued, has one key difference. Contemporary hyper-flexible and precarious work, it is argued, is largely a matter of individual choice. This was not the case in feudal England, villeins were little more than slaves to the landowner whose position was given by the king whose own position was divinely appointed. The weight behind the economic arrangements of the time was not simply the market, but religious and regal. The medieval mind did not allow for questioning the feudal system because it was rooted in religion and the monarchy, this arrangement was God's Will.

Now, and since the Enlightenment in the West, we have largely jettisoned religious explanations and prescriptions for life in favour of a scientific understanding and the social relations between us are also less obviously influenced by religious doctrines. While the medieval mind took social relations to be God's Will and therefore little to do with choice, the argument put before us with regard to the gig economy is that those engaged in such work have a choice, and this is bound up with the notion of flexible working. There remains, however, the question of whether a contemporary gig economy worker actually has this choice, a point to which we will return later in the book.

The relationship between stakeholders in the gig economy is also served well by another use of the word gig, as part of the word "gigolo". The gigolo is a male escort or social companion who is supported by a woman in a continuing relationship, often living in her residence or having to be present at her beck and call.[3] It is this latter connotation that matters, as we shall see, the gig worker is usually required to be at the beck and call of the "employer". The relationship is seen as transactional, but is it equal? Needless to say, companies pursuing this form of labour arrangement argue that the people they pay to do this type of work are able to choose whether or not to carry out these very short-term contracts; for them the arrangement is one in which two parties agree on a contract freely and may opt out of such contracts in the future. The appeal is therefore to the notion of the market as a place where all parties are in some way equal, at least in as far as they are "free to choose" (Friedman 1979). But are they free to choose? Are drivers and people on bicycles delivering small items from a box strapped to their back actually free to opt out of that arrangement? Would the phone stop ringing or text messages offering them a new gig dry up if they were rejected too often?

The notion of the free market may also need questioning (as it has been for a very long time). Such an idea suggests a level of equality between the different parties. Yet this is very unlikely, as Adam Smith was well aware in the eighteenth century: "people of the same trade seldom meet together, even for merriment and diversion, but the conversation ends in a conspiracy against the public, or in some contrivance to raise prices" (Smith 1776/1982).

Large corporations have more information and more information processing capacity; they can buy that intelligence, to which the driver or delivery person does not have access. Many would argue it is not a perfect market

---

3. See https://www.thefreedictionary.com/gigolo (accessed 16 October 2018).

as there is no perfect information. Yet, they point out, we continue to adhere slavishly to the central tenets of the free market economy. Does the market really provide as equally as this, or is it really in favour of the big corporation? These questions will be addressed later in the book.

Given the nature of the relationship between the gig company and the gig worker as presented above one of the casualties of the gig economy might be the notion of loyalty. The idea of "jobs for life", often associated with working in a government function such as the post office (GPO), is a thing of the past. The phrase "job for life" would often be accompanied by the phrase "set for life" implying that once such a job had been landed so your employment worries were over until retirement. There was, in these jobs, the sense that you would be "looked after" by a paternalistic company. In return for your loyalty you could expect security of employment, a gold watch after a lifetime's service and a final salary pension on retirement. This security would be seen as highly prized following the leaner years before, between and during the two world wars. The notion of reciprocated loyalty may have been somewhat romanticized, but it was not an uncommon experience for the baby-boomer generation. However, their children were to be disappointed as government jobs and public providers became commercial concerns with as much propensity to lay people off as any commercial company. The company's reduced sense of loyalty to employees was further demonstrated in the 1980s following the decimation of the trades unions.

Conclusion

This brief survey of the uses of the word "gig" has illuminated the key features of gig work, the gig worker and the relationship between them. Gig work is precarious, infrequent, badly paid, unstable and fortuitous, while the gig–work relationship is seen as transactional but unequal. Perhaps one of the most striking features of the use of the word "gig" is its warm familiarity. It conveys a lightness of activity, frivolity and even humour. The Oxford English Dictionary has an entry that defines the gig as a joke or merriment. Images abound of the bohemian musician living from day to day, grateful for the next gig, frequently out of work yet glad to be outside the strictures of "normal" society. In turn, proponents of the gig economy have argued that these arrangements "free" workers from the strictures of traditional internal labour markets and hence forces greater competition by employers (Friedman 2014a, 2014b).

Other phrases have surfaced to bolster the euphemistic tone and user-friendly poetry of the term gig economy. For example, there is "flexible working" – a catch-all term covering practices that can denote any deviation from a rigidly defined working week and is linked with work–life balance (Kelliher & Anderson 2010). There is also the "sharing economy" (Zervas *et al.* 2017), incorporating online platforms such as Airbnb, whereby individuals can "make use of under-utilized inventory by fee-based sharing" (*ibid.*: 687). However, we would argue that this is a somewhat different concept to that of the gig economy as it essentially facilitates consumer-to-consumer (C2C) transactions without the need for any paid labour intermediation. We also have the "freelance economy" (Kuhn 2016), "hyper-flexible" work (Harvey *et al.* 2017), and "unicorn" companies: high-tech (typically software/IT) companies, often emergent and with high market capitalization (Simon 2016).

Counter to these are terms that refer to less desirable characteristics associated with the gig economy; for example, "zero-hours contracts" (Brinkley 2013) and "precarious work" (Campbell & Price 2016), emphasizing its ubiquitous, yet highly contingent indeterminate nature, its clandestine connotations, and its less-than-amiable implications for working people. What is new is the idea that the entire economic structure of society is now predicated on the existence of a highly flexible workforce, and on companies being able to decide what their labour needs are within a very short time frame. This was a clear aim of the Cameron Government from 2010 to 2016; with its continued belief that a deregulated labour market (Williams & Scott 2010) would ultimately make the UK more competitive. It referenced the "gig economy" because it had moved from being sporadic and fragmented to being a structural element of contemporary society.

Outline of the book

Following this opening chapter, the book proceeds in Chapter 2 with a survey of the theoretical contributions to the gig economy. This chapter provides the conceptual foundations for understanding the dynamics of the labour market in the gig economy. It is not intended to provide an exhaustive account of theories pertaining to work and employment but rather to consider the impact of labour flexibility on economic and societal outcomes. Chapter 2 commences with a review of the simple partial equilibrium neoclassical model of the labour market and then considers how feasible such markets are in practice. This review is then followed with a historical overview of the literature on segmented labour markets, labour flexibility and more recent literature on organizational forms and the impact of globalization on labour flexibility. Both supply-side factors and demand-side factors are considered in analyzing the growth of work in the gig economy.

Chapter 3 delineates evidence for the gig economy by grounding the concept of gig work in the conventional lexicon of flexible work forms. Four categories of work and employment are considered here as being typical of the gig economy: casual work, temporary agency work, zero-hours contracts, and dependent contractors. We argue that these forms of work are largely coterminous with the gig economy, as they are characterized by a high degree of flexibility and hence volatility of hours worked; have little to no employment protections (with dependent contractors not being considered as employees); and are characterized by a highly unequal bargaining relationship where work schedules are largely controlled by the employer (often to the exclusion of being able to undertake work for others whilst "on-call"). Chapter 3 assess the extent of these forms of work, and appraises the arguments put forward for their growth, taking in both developed and emerging economies.

Chapter 4 then examines the issues surrounding regulation of the forms of work denoted in Chapter 3. The key issue that arises here is that the labour regulations framework across countries has developed in accordance with the pursuit of the standard employment relationship (SER), i.e., permanent full-time employment. As non-standard forms of work have grown, so the regulatory coverage has diminished, prompting regulatory catch-up by authorities seeking to promote equal treatment of non-standard workers and thereby extend employment rights. Chapter 4 concludes by exploring the "lived experience" of gig workers and considers the challenges that gig work poses for an agenda of "decent work".

The concluding chapter (Chapter 5) considers wider issues relating to the advent of the gig economy and the implications for society as a whole. Key here have been arguments around the underpinning role of technology as driving developments in the sector, and the attendant potential for artificial intelligence (AI) and automation to radically redesign jobs and work regimes still further. We also critically consider the notion that the market should be of prime status in how work is mediated. This in turn raises profound questions relating to the efficacy of gig work becoming a structural part of society and the world of work.

2

Theorizing the gig economy

The previous chapter has highlighted the origin and context of work associated with the gig economy. Apparent is that for the majority of the age of capitalism, work has been associated with commodification of labour. In this sense, the shift to the cities with industrialization in Europe was characterized by a breakdown of the traditional hierarchical relationships between landowners and peasants associated with feudalism. Such work relationships featured some degree of reciprocity and long-term expectations between the different social classes – although, unequal and often violent, as they were. In this sense, as Thomas Hobbes wrote in *Leviathan* in 1651 (Hobbes 2008) life was "nasty, brutish and short".[4] However, industrialization saw the emergence of an urban proletariat in work characterized by alienation and exploitation (Thompson 1963). Work in the eighteenth and early nineteenth centuries was characterized by long hours, low wages and relative ease of hiring and firing. Hence, work was highly precarious, and workers could be easily dismissed and replaced, with the presence of a "reserve army" of the unemployed serving to moderate worker demands (Marx 1887/2018).

However, the increasing organization of the working class and rising affluence throughout the course of the late nineteenth century – and hence the emergence of social democratic parties in Europe and its colonial offshoots – served to usher in policies that promoted increasing regulation and welfare at work. The earliest regulations on the employment relationship in industrialized economies consisted of limitations on the working day and eliminating the "worst forms" of labour, such as child labour and women in certain occupations, such as coal mining (De Ruyter *et al.* 2011). However, by

---

4. George Orwell acerbically put it in his novel *Nineteen Eighty-Four*, that this harsh existence was only softened by a notion of "promises of compensation in some imaginary world beyond the grave".

the early twentieth century, in the UK for example, the Liberal government in 1906 had recognized the "right to strike" and introduced unemployment insurance and old age pensions (Birch 1998). This was also accompanied by shifts in production techniques that recognized that well-paid workers with some modicum of job security were more productive workers; most notably epitomized in Henry Ford's pioneering of the automotive assembly line and paying his workers good wages.

It was in this period that the emergence of a more affluent white, male working class began to take shape. This depiction is not unimportant, as social democratic parties could also be nationalist and patriarchal parties, defining their community of interests along ethnic and gender lines. For example, in Australia, the cornerstone of the industrial settlement between capital and labour that emerged – supported by the Australian Labor Party at the time – also emphasized protectionist trade policies, an inferior wage position for women (who were expected to marry and withdraw from the labour force) and a "White Australia" immigration policy. This settlement lasted until the 1970s; and broke down only amidst the more general crisis encompassing western economies at the time.

Theory of the firm

The thrust of development of capitalist economies in the course of the early twentieth century favoured the emergence of larger corporate organizational units that increasingly substituted market-based relationships with more long-tern employment relationships. These larger units of production could attain substantial economies of scale and thereby reduce costs. The experience of the Great Depression in the 1930s and the rise of totalitarian regimes in many countries carried this process still further and the sobering experience of the Second World War ushered in the welfare state in western capitalist economies.

In seeking to explain these developments, economists began to focus on industrial organization in an attempt to explain why firms would prefer internal employment relationships over market-based relationships. Ronald Coase, in 1937, famously identified that a key factor that lead to firms recognizing the advantages of having a stable workforce of employees lay in the notion of transaction costs:

It may be desired to make a long-term contract for the supply of some article or service. This may be due to the fact that if one contract is made for a longer period, instead of several shorter ones, then certain costs of making each contract will be avoided. ... It is obviously of more importance in the case of services – labour, than it is in the case of the buying of commodities" (Coase 1937: 391–2).

In Coase's theory of the firm, firms existed because internalizing transactions meant that savings could be made on repeated contracting on the open market. Such transaction costs could include search costs, hiring costs and costs of training. For Coase, the optimal firm size was one where the internal costs of coordinating production would be no more than the costs of contracting on the external market – a development that favoured larger oligopolistic units given their significant economies of scale. In positing the existence of significant transaction costs, Coase exposed a key deficiency of the simple neoclassical model of the labour market, which posited perfect competition, no barriers to entry and exit, homogenous labour and complete information. To posit the existence of transaction costs then, was to acknowledge that markets had explicit temporal and spatial dimensions and were rarely (if ever) characterized by complete information and frictionless movement of the various factors of production.

However, other economists and social theorists, focusing on the interaction between firms and wider society, emphasized the role of institutions and "collective action" during the 1930s and 1940s in explaining the emergence of firms characterized by internal labour markets. In this vein, John Commons – a key figure amongst American institutional economists – writing in 1931, presaged the literature on internal labour markets by commenting that the employment relationship (as an "economic relationship") was subject to the influence of a number of parties:

Either the state, or a corporation, or a cartel, or a holding company, or a cooperative association, or a trade union, or an employers' association, or a trade association, or a joint trade agreement of two associations, or a stock exchange, or a board of trade, may *lay down and enforce the rules* which determine for individuals this bundle of correlative and reciprocal economic relationships (Commons 1931: 2, emphasis added).

For Commons then, the employment relationship represented a distinct departure from short-term contractual market relations and the price mechanism, and was the outcome of the interaction of the institutions denoted. Similarly, Clark Kerr, writing in 1954, explicitly argued that the activities of unions were instrumental in the "institutionalisation of labour markets" (Kerr 1954: 96). With the enacting of the welfare state and Keynesian macroeconomic policies in capitalist economies after 1945, the role of the state expanded significantly. This was particularly notable in the commitment to full employment that enabled the widespread development of internalized employment relationships in firms, as depicted by internal labour markets (Standing 1997). Hence, it is to these institutions that we now turn.

Internal labour markets

If the external labour market could be regarded as the simple competitive labour market depicted in the basic neoclassical model, then internal labour markets could be regarded as structured (and essentially, not characterized by open competition). The major characteristic of internal labour markets, in accordance with Commons' view, is that the matching of labour supply and demand and wage determination is enabled according to a set of administrative rules (Norris 1983), rather than relying on an external price mechanism. As such, they are not open to competition from outsiders at all, so long as an incumbent generally performs satisfactorily. Vacancies are filled by internal promotion through job ladders, with the exception of entry-level positions, known as "ports of entry" (*ibid.*: 81). In this sense, they are arguably not markets at all, but a different kind of institution (Marsden 1986). It could be argued that the distinction between the internal labour market and the external labour market could be regarded as the simplest example of segmented labour markets (see next section).

However, there is no *a priori* reason as to why the existence of internal labour markets should imply the existence of a corresponding external labour market, or segmentation as such. It is quite feasible that an entire workforce could be covered by internal arrangements. This could occur, for example, when the government provides a set of administrative rules to regulate job-matching, and wage determination and the education system links directly into ports of entry. However, in practice, it is improbable that internal labour markets would cover the entire workforce, although for the postwar period (until about 1980) they covered the majority of workers in OECD countries.

Internal labour markets can be classified according to the types of administrative rules in place. Kerr (1954), wrote of the "Balkanization" of labour markets. He argued that the labour market could be divided into three categories: general/competitive labour markets; craft/guild labour markets, and enterprise/manorial labour markets. In craft labour markets, general training was important and skills were recognized through certificates, for example, apprenticeships. Workers in craft labour markets displayed a high degree of mobility between firms, and seniority was related to experience in one's occupation, rather than time spent with any individual firm. In contrast, enterprise labour markets were closed, with well-defined job ladders and few ports of entry. It was also possible to stipulate the existence of "open" internal labour markets that were characterized by ports of entry at all job classification levels. These structures differed from competitive labour markers only in the sense that incumbents generally had seniority rights over would-be replacements (cited in Norris 1983: 89–90).

Also associated with internal labour markets was the "job competition model", as developed by Lester Thurow (1976; cited in Thurow 1996: 179). In this model, firms' recruitment practices would be based upon the amount of training they would be required to "invest" in potential employees. Since firms could not easily ascertain the abilities of potential employees, they would be forced to assess job applicants on the basis of desired characteristics, such as education, sex, age or union affiliation. Education would be used as a screening device, as an indicator of the ability to undertake training. Thus workers would enter the labour market with a set of skills and then compete with each other on the basis of what wage they would accept. The best jobs would then go to those with the most desired characteristics (notwithstanding the attendant potential for discrimination that selection on the basis of personal characteristics could entail). In contrast, those with the least desirable characteristics would fall to the end of the job queue, and hence have access only to low-paying jobs and the prospect of intermittent unemployment.

Turning to the evolution of internal labour markets, a number of explanations have been put forward as to how these institutions developed. Doeringer and Piore (1971), echoing Coase, argued in neoclassical fashion that internal labour markets could "logically" develop from competitive labour markets, as firms sought to minimize the transaction costs associated with externalized training arrangements. Thus, an internal labour market would be bound by the limits of the enterprise. The emergence of firm-specific skills would then be seen as the major catalyst for the development of an internal labour market. Oliver Williamson (1985) extended this approach under the rubric of "transaction cost economics". For Williamson, the primary reason for the emergence of organizations was the need to economize on transaction costs. However, in moving beyond Coase's analysis, Williamson incorporated aspects of Herbert Simon's (1958; cited in Simon 1997) notion of bounded rationality, and also elements of human capital theory (Becker 1964).

Transaction costs give rise to the need for governance structures, all the more important since economic agents are assumed to adhere to a strong form of self-interest, referred to as opportunism (Williamson 1985: 47). Opportunism entails the possibility of exploiting agreements by either party to a contract, should the chance arise. In the labour market, this could manifest in employees "shirking" after getting a job, or employers reneging on a collective bargaining agreement. Measures are then needed to counter opportunistic behaviour. The nature of agreements would then be primarily affected by "asset specificity" (*ibid.*: 30), whereby transactions requiring substantial investments by both employer and employee would engender the basis for a long-term employment relationship.

Segmented labour markets

Segmentation of the labour market can be defined as the process whereby the labour market becomes separated into distinct groups between which there is little or no movement. This process might represent the influence of gender and race factors, or alternatively represent attempts by employers to divide the workforce. The emergence of segmentation theories can be traced back to the nineteenth century, with the writings of classical economists such as John Cairnes, who wrote of "non-competing groups". In Cairnes' schema, the labour market was characterized by competition within, but not between, different groups (Marsden 1986: 142). This represented a clear departure from the simple neoclassical model of the labour market which assumed that all labour was homogenous.

Segmentation highlights the role that personal characteristics, opportunity, luck and non-competitive conditions can have in determining labour market outcomes. For example, it has been evidenced that there have been different returns to labour based on race and gender (Preston 1997). In addition, rates can differ across occupation, industry and location according to different degrees of monopoly and monopsony power in labour markets and different degrees of monopoly in product markets (*ibid.*).

Broadly speaking, segmentation theories tend to fall into two categories. The first, representing the so-called "new institutional economics" were posited around the notion of transaction costs and firm-specific skills referred to earlier. Notable contributors in this tradition include Doeringer and Piore (1971), Williamson (1985) and Lepak and Snell (1999). In depicting segmentation as the outcome of a rational economic process, such theories represented only a trivial departure from the basic axioms of neoclassical economics. In such schemas, the role of worker organizations in the development of segmented labour markets is given scant attention. The second category built on the work of traditional institutional economists such as John Commons to articulate a wider range of economic and social factors in having shaped segmentation. Whilst much of the labour market segmentation literature displays a narrow focus on manufacturing and/or large firms (e.g., Atkinson 1984), it still forms a useful body of work to adduce the institutional features of capitalism, and hence the pressures that have contributed to organizational change and the consequent growth of the gig economy.

The dual labour market hypothesis, as developed by Doeringer and Piore (1971), is the simplest example of labour market segmentation. The labour market here is separated into a primary sector and a secondary sector, with the partition generally determined by industry structure. The primary sector generally consisted of firms with a high degree of monopoly power in their product markets. Norris (1983: 108) notes that the primary sector typically consisted of oligopolistic firms operating in sectors such as manufacturing, transport, utilities and the public sector. Such firms typically had manorial internal labour markets characterized by administrative rules (echoing Kerr), high wages, secure permanent (usually full-time) employment, training and career development based on seniority amongst employees – and, strong trade unions which could negotiate "closed shop"[5] arrangements with management (*ibid.*).

In contrast, the secondary sector was characterized by lower wages, a high degree of precarious employment and hence a marked absence of training and career opportunities, and by little, or no, union representation. The secondary sector then, was characterized by an employment relationship that was short-termist in its orientation; where there was little manifest desire by employers to offer permanent employment, or an expectation by workers of such arrangements thereof. Firms operating in the secondary sector, then, typically exhibited high labour turnover (*ibid.*).

However, in practice (a typical problem with dualistic typologies of the labour market), identifying which firms or industries or types of employment belong to the primary or secondary sector can be operationally problematic. It could be argued that small firms would be part of the secondary sector, as they face tighter cash flows, generally have less market power and hence are exposed to higher risk – and as such more likely to engage in short-term cost minimizing approaches to managing operations that would indicate a high use of precarious (low wage) forms of work. However, such a demarcation represents a crude proxy at best, as small firms might themselves occupy niche areas that convey some degree of innovatory capacity, market power and hence longer-term commitment to workers as employees. Equally, large firms might also engage in cost-minimizing approaches to operational management that lend themselves to the significant use of precarious forms of work. As such, a clear-cut distinction between "primary" and "secondary" sectors is hard to support in practice. Inferior jobs occur amongst and within all industries and occupational groups, reflecting the fact that firms can segment their own workers into "good" and "bad" jobs (a point taken up by later segmentation theorists, as will be seen in subsequent chapters).

Also important to the validity of the dual labour market hypothesis is that technology is assigned as the primary determinant of employment distribution, in that the primary sector is characterized by the need for skilled workers, particularly those with firm-specific skills. Hence, a long-term

---

5. A "closed shop" referred to an industrial relations configuration whereby all workers employed by a firm had to join a trade union.

employment relationship (cf. Williamson) is derived by the need to accommodate workers with firm-specific skills that have been invested in via substantial training. With technological advancement, then, the primary sector should expand as more skilled positions are needed (Rubery 1978).

However, it is not apparent that improved technology should necessarily result in the need for a more skilled workforce. Harry Braverman, writing in 1974, argued that technological change, in contradistinction to the dual labour market hypothesis, could actually *de-skill* the workforce, and hence lead to an expansion of the secondary sector. This was because technological advancement typically served to automate production processes that previously had required complex mechanical knowledge and manual procedures. This argument is not unimportant in present-day discourses around the gig economy, as technology has been seen as a driving factor in simplifying formerly complex processes, reducing the need for human cognition and manual input. It has also served to automate the job matching function, through the use of online platforms such as "work on demand apps" (De Stefano 2016), which reduce job search and matching costs to firms. This has reduced the requirement for skilled workers – and in turn the need for a regular employment relationship to accommodate such workers. Hence, technological advancement, rather than de-commodifying labour, can serve to recommodify it (see De Stefano 2016, for a discussion on this pertaining to the gig economy). The issues surrounding the growth of such work are depicted in Box 2.1 overleaf.

Braverman's critique of technological change as necessarily being a benign force serving to improve the nature of the labour market for workers is important, particularly in the current context of the growth of the gig economy – a theme that is returned to in subsequent chapters of this book. However, there are also other factors at play that have been ignored in simple segmentation theories.

The labour market segmentation theories described above highlight the important issue of organizational and management practices in shaping how the labour market functions. However, in attempting to explain segmentation along strict industry or occupational lines, such theories have failed to adequately address the dynamic forces (structural and institutional) that serve to shape labour market outcomes. In particular, such theories have understated the impact of the state of the external labour market on internal labour markets (Grimshaw & Rubery 1998). In addition, the impact of

---

BOX 2.1 THE DRIVERS OF THE GIG ECONOMY

While the essential features of the gig economy have been with us since medieval times, (Geraint *et al.* 2017), the reasons for the current explosion in gig work appear to revolve around technology and lifestyle changes. Exactly which came first is a "chicken and egg" discussion and probably not useful. Nevertheless, it is apparent that hundreds of millions of people now carry quite astonishing technology around in their back pockets and, via the "app", we are now able to do much more and quickly. Ordering a taxi, for example, involves being able to watch its journey on screen as it turns corners on its way to pick us up, thereby blurring the lines between functionality and entertainment. This is a result of smartphones, satellites and GPS and inevitably companies are keen to exploit this technology for profit. The second clear driver of this is lifestyle changes. We can work now from almost anywhere and companies are happy to make use of this too. Providing a work space is confining, expensive and potentially counterproductive. Companies are able to "allow" their employees to work in their own time, but also in their own homes, which has implications for the cost of providing a workspace and workers can be monitored in myriad ways without the necessity of their physical presence. But as we answer emails and much more at any time of the day or night, some workers are now claiming that time spent working, for example, on public transport to and from work should be paid for (BBC News, 30 August 2018). Given the pace of change in technology we might well ask "where will this go next?" but the concern for many is the extent to which the technology controls the people rather than the other way around.

---

changes in the structure of firms on the development of firm-specific skills is not adequately considered (Marsden 1986). A general skill could become firm-specific if a firm attains a position of monopsony in the labour market for that skill, for example, the UK coal industry after nationalization in 1945 (*ibid.* 155).

Hence, labour market segmentation is prone to change over time and in this sense, is periodically re-segmented (Brosnan 1996). The role of aggregate demand is crucial to determining the nature of worker segmentation. As output and employment increase, firms are forced to hire from less desirable sections of the labour force. This would tend to alter the pattern of segmentation, unless the "structure of jobs is re-segmented so that the new source of labour can be hired under different terms from the existing workers" (*ibid.* 155). In a similar vein, the impact of unemployment on the composition of the labour market, and on management practices, is given scant attention.

Various theorists have attempted to deal with these objections. Gordon (1972; cited in Rubery 1978), writing from a Marxist labour process theory perspective, argued that the dual labour market arises as the outcome of deliberate management attempts to maintain control over the workforce, in order to prevent the labour homogenization necessary to carry out the class struggle. Segmentation then maintains division through the creation of job ladders and worker rivalry ("divide and conquer"). In this schema, a secondary sector characterized by precarious work can be seen to enable control in both sectors.

However, Hyman (1987) argued that segmentation arose not for reasons of control, but rather the desire by management to stabilize the workforce, particularly those with scarce attributes that helped lower recruitment and training costs. Whilst at first glance this might seem like a reprise of the idea that firm-specific skills lead to labour market segmentation, Hyman actually highlights that *worker power*, rather than management power, can lead to labour market segmentation. In other words, segmentation arises not for reasons of control, but rather the need to accommodate the "expectations and *disruptive potential* of strategically placed occupational groups" (*ibid.* 39; emphasis added). This represents a clear departure from the view espoused in the dual labour market hypothesis that management are the sole progenitor of internalized labour market arrangements.

These arguments hence encapsulate a wider view than that of simply positing internal and segmented labour markets as arising due to management initiatives to retain workers with firm-specific skills. However, it could be argued that even these theorists do not give enough attention to the dynamics of how segmentation could adjust over time. Indeed, the process of labour market segmentation is presented as monotonic and invariant over time. In contrast, Sengenberger (1981) outlined a case for arguing that the state of the business cycle does have a pervasive impact on the nature of labour market segmentation, vis-à-vis labour and management strategies. Specifically: "[i]n general terms it may be hypothesized that labour market strategies which create barriers to flexibility by restricting mobility and/ or substitutability are developed by that part of the labour market whose interests are most endangered when competition amongst its own members increases" (*ibid*.: 256).

The implication of this argument is that employees/unions will try to reinforce segmentation when unemployment is high (*ibid*.). In slack labour markets, the presence of internal labour markets can reduce the effectiveness of the industrial reserve mechanism as a disciplining tool for capitalists.[6] This occurs because worker substitutability could be impeded by firm-specific skills or statutes that preserve practices such as "last on first off". In contrast, for those in the secondary sector, there is the potential for the creation of disenfranchised groups of workers (employed and unemployed) not subject to the benefits of being part of an internal labour market – a group whose numbers could increase during an economic downturn. It should not be assumed that this would necessarily be an invariant proposition in itself. Custom and societal norms could impinge on the actions undertaken by some firms. Similarly (as Sengenberger highlights), the actions of labour will be constrained by trade union structure and practices within a country (*ibid*.: 257).

However, Sengenberger highlighted how labour market segmentation is sensitive to the overall level of unemployment. Moreover, he articulated that the strategies pursued by capital and labour can change over the course of a business cycle, even to the point where the original strategy becomes anachronistic. This could be seen through the initial endorsement of enterprise-level collective bargaining by the majority of the Australian trade union movement in the early 1990s, through to its reaffirmation of centralized wage determination as the inequities of enterprise bargaining wage outcomes became apparent during the 1990s. It could also be seen in the "traditional swing in popularity that the [Australian] arbitration and conciliation system enjoyed over the business cycle" (Brosnan *et al.* 1992: 22). The Australian system worked to the advantage of employers during economic upswings because of the moderating ability on wage levels that a centralized system had, leading to union dissatisfaction. Conversely, during

---

6. The concept of an industrial reserve army was first articulated by Marx (1887/2018), as a means for capital(ists) to drive down the wages and conditions of labour. The industrial reserve mechanism is the means by which capital exerts power over labour by the threat of substituting existing employees with the unemployed, should the demands of labour become intolerable.

economic downturns, wage levels would remain above those encountered in more market-regulated systems, thereby leading to employer dissatisfaction with the arbitration system (*ibid.*).

Thus, it is possible to conceive of labour market segmentation as arising from convergent strategies by firms for example (Rubery 1994; cited in McNabb & Whitfield 1998: 348). This point is developed further by Grimshaw and Rubery (1998: 212), who argued that "it is necessary to address how external and internal competitive pressures mutually interact upon firms and to assess the implications for different groups of workers".

Finally, the actions of institutions not directly involved in the labour market should also be considered in creating and maintaining segmentation. Of course, the actions of government as an external body are pivotal to this process – indeed, as an employer in its own right the government can directly create and shape internal labour market structures; as depicted in its post-Second World War role as a model employer. In contrast, from the 1980s onwards in many countries, government moves to substitute state regulation with market regulation resulted in increased competition in product markets, which in turn has affected the behaviour of capital (increasingly international capital) and labour over the business cycle. The historical role of government in providing education for the development of firm-specific skills through the apprenticeship system should not be underestimated (Marsden 1986). Indeed, associated with the decline of internal labour market mechanisms with the shift to a more neoliberal policy regime has been the severely diminished role of government in the apprenticeship system. This has occurred as governments have privatized state-owned firms and opened up the economy to increased international competition.

The role of government in creating nationwide wage and job classifications (*ibid.*) demonstrates the creation of structures associated with internal labour markets that extend beyond the individual firm, as depicted in the Doeringer and Piore (1971) model. In this sense, the widespread adoption of internal labour market structures and the consequent literature on segmented labour markets with the attendant notion of a (diminishing) secondary sector, can be seen principally as having been facilitated by the actions of government. It is no coincidence that the spread of internal labour markets occurred strongly in the postwar period of nationalization of key industries, the expansion of the welfare state and a commitment to full employment at the macroeconomic level. It was during this period that the balance between capital and labour was altered so as to mitigate the experience of the interwar period of high unemployment that favoured externalized work arrangements (Standing 1997), and hence favoured the dominance of the (permanent full-time) standard employment relationship, or SER (Bosch 2004).

The transformation of the internal labour market?
Labour flexibility in the era of globalization

In contrast to the thirty years immediately after the Second World War, typified by the employment arrangements described in the previous section, the labour market since 1980 in mature capitalist economies has been characterized by fragmentation and atomization. At the macroeconomic level, the period since 1980 (and particularly after the end of the Cold War) has been typified by globalization, the spread of market regulation and the rise to dominance of transnational firms, and foreign direct investment-led economic development. In turn there has been a resultant growth in the "precariat" (Standing 1997, 2011) across all countries and sectors – in manufacturing as well as services, in the public sector as well as the private sector. Can high unemployment (relative to the period 1945–75), global production networks, the increasing prevalence of "non-standard" employment, declining employment security, falling trade union densities across most countries, and the emergence of ambiguous forms of work typified by the gig economy really be seen as a manifestation of the demise of internal labour markets? Or has re-institutionalization and re-segmentation of the labour market occurred within and across countries?

As such, these developments pose a challenge to labour market segmentation theorists. Labour force fragmentation (Caire 1989; Standing 1997) is a process whereby the workforce becomes divided into groups characterized by some degree of antagonism (e.g., workers in mature industrial economies against those in emerging economies as processes of globalization have unfolded). Atomization refers to a breakdown of collective institutions regulating the labour market and consequent replacement with an individualized system of worker relations. Standing (1997) provides a useful taxonomy that depicts how workers can be fragmented into a hierarchy of groups, including the unemployed and those deemed "economically inactive" (as shown in Figure 2.1).

At the apex of the hierarchy are a small group of extremely well-paid globe-trotters employed as senior managers and executives, often on fixed-term contracts. These are followed by the conventional standard employment salariat, concentrated in professional and administrative occupations. Below the salariat come a group referred to by Standing as "proficians". Proficians are workers with specific skills, typically hired for a finite basis linked to a particular project or otherwise a fixed-term contract. These employees are usually found in professional and para-professional (white-collar) jobs. Below these come the traditional working class, employed on a traditional open-ended (standard) contract – an ever-shrinking group prevalent in blue-collar occupations. Below these are a group referred to as "flexiworkers", otherwise known as the "precariat"; mainly service-sector workers in precarious jobs, many of whom move either between such jobs or otherwise face spells of intermittent employment alternating with unemployment or economic inactivity (shown in Figure 2.1 by some degree of movement between the lower levels in the hierarchy). Lastly come the unemployed and economically inactive at the bottom of the hierarchy. In this schema, only the salariat and traditional working class could be considered

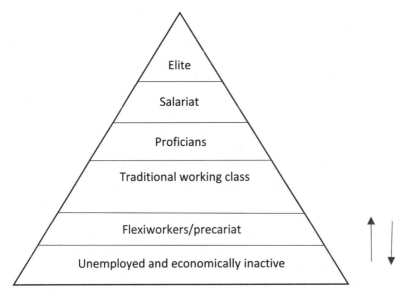

Figure 2.1 A hierarchy of workers

as being in a SER. Flexiworkers in contrast, can be considered as a key element of the gig economy, given its contingent nature (the same could also be said of proficians to a degree, in that they could be synonymous with "freelancers").

Increasing fragmentation of the workforce poses implications for the traditional distinction between "employed" and "employee", as the distinction between the two is no longer clear-cut. This is particularly evident in considering the nature of "self-employment", and, as noted in previous sections, to be "self-employed" is one of the keynote characteristics of the gig economy. Traditionally, to be self-employed has been to be considered as an independent contractor, or even, an "entrepreneur" or a "business person". However, workers in the gig economy tend to only work for one company, and thus would fall under the category of "dependent contractor".

This distinction is not unimportant, as historically, the umbrella of protective employment regulation in mature industrial economies, such as the UK, which developed over the course of the twentieth century only covered workers designated as "employees". Hence, the consequent employment relationship would be depicted in terms of being accompanied by a platform of rights for the worker and responsibilities from the employer. In this sense, the thrust of EU employment directives over the past 20 years has been to extend the working conditions of standard (i.e., permanent full-time) employees to non-standard (e.g., part-time, fixed-term and agency) employees.

The self-employed in contrast, have been excluded from this because they have been assumed not to have an employment relationship with clients. That the self-employed only constituted 10 per cent or so of the workforce in countries such as the UK in the postwar period only reinforced their depiction of being part of a residual, secondary sector and hence largely outside the purview of those interested in promoting labour standards and regulation. However, the growth of such forms of work in recent years (i.e., since the 2008 crisis) has posed major challenges for the labour regulation system, based as it is on the notion of waged employment. As such, the proliferation of ambiguous forms of work as epitomizing a departure from common law has increasingly called into question "the contract of employment as a normative reference point" in itself (Caire 1989: 102). At a conceptual level, such forms of work also further serve to erode the distinction between the internal and external labour market. For some authors, such developments have suggested a shift to a core–periphery workforce, employed within a "flexible firm". As such discussions around labour flexibility have been highly influential in the labour market literature, it is worth consider the premises of this model.

The flexible firm

First articulated by John Atkinson in 1984, the core–periphery model of the firm (in essence an adaptation of the dual labour market hypothesis), also known as the "flexible firm" denoted a radical departure from the previous literature on labour market segmentation in that it posited that labour market segmentation could take place *within* a firm, and hence that a firm could pursue different human resources strategies (strategic HRM) for different groups of workers. Products and technology were taken as given and the firm would focus its efforts on cost adjustments (Wilkinson & White 1994).

In this model, the "primary sector" consisted of a core workforce of employees displaying "functional flexibility" (i.e., multi-skilled, so able to operate across different areas of production), also referred to as job broadening, or polyvalence (Allan *et al.* 1999). For these employees, career development meant the continual acquisition of new skills (*ibid.*). The "secondary sector" consisted of a workforce of peripheral employees displaying "financial flexibility", i.e., they were subject to the ability of the firm to adjust their costs, including wages. Peripheral employees also were characterized by "numerical flexibility" (i.e., subject to the firm's ability to adjust workforce numbers, or hours worked, in response to fluctuations in demand). A similar concept is "temporal flexibility", which entails the ability of management to adjust working-time to demand patterns (Deery & Mahony 1994). Peripheral employees typically were low-skilled and had little access to training and career paths, or they were individuals whose skills were not specific to the firm.

Later versions of the model (Atkinson 1987) added a third tier of workers (contractors, or consultants as part of an "external sector") denoted under the label of "distancing" – that is, the substitution of employment relationships by commercial relationships. Other variants of this model further specify additional types of flexibility, such as "procedural flexibility" or "techno-organizational flexibility" (Rimmer & Zappala 1988; cited in Allan

1999: 136). In so doing, the flexible firm model explicitly links job content to employment status.

However, the flexible firm model has been widely criticized on theoretical and empirical grounds. The model suffered from a problem of definitional clarity in that it was unclear whether it was descriptive, or predictive (Burgess 1995). Atkinson himself, in response to such criticisms that only a small proportion of firms could be said to be consciously pursuing a core–periphery strategy, said that the model described "tendencies" in the workforce (1987: 94). Some critics suggested that the model also appears prescriptive, given its emphasis on labour flexibility. Burgess (1997: 89) suggested that the model appeared as something firms should pursue, whilst Campbell (1993) argued that the attainment of "increased flexibility" was used as a rallying cry by those calling for more substitution of state regulation by market regulation.

The flexible firm model is also restricted in that it only described large firms operating in the private sector. This leaves it with a weak epistemological base, given that it was formulated primarily on the basis of surveys with large firms in the manufacturing sector (Burgess 1997). However, the majority of what could be described as peripheral employment "growth" has taken place in SMEs and in the services sector. In these firms, no clear-cut distinction between core and periphery employees exists. In the hospitality industry, for example, casual and agency workers are regularly used to provide core services (*ibid.*). This highlights the operational problem of actually trying to identify/designate core and peripheral employees in the economy. The dualistic division of workers into core and periphery also overlooks the fact that core workers could themselves be segmented, with some groups of workers displaying periphery characteristics. For Cappelli (1995), the types of changes that were occurring in labour markets in industrialized economies at the time did denote a breakdown of internal labour market structures, but not just in the growth of non-standard employment, but in changes that also affected permanent employees (*ibid.*).

Cognizant of this, a more recent version of the flexible firm typology can be found in Lepak and Snell's (1999) "human resources architectures" framework, which combines human capital and resource-based views of the firm (building on Williamson's approach to transaction costs). This typology suggests that firms would only pursue long-term commitment relationships with workers that demonstrate both high "value" of human capital, and high "uniqueness" of human capital. More explicitly than in Atkinson's model, the emphasis here is clearly on strategic intent. In this context it is the uniqueness and value of human capital that will dictate which workers are taken on as permanent employees (*ibid.*). Employers thus, would utilize external contracting in instances where skill-specificity to the organization is lacking. Such a combination can be seen in the engagement of external consultants for IT (high value, low uniqueness); or agency workers for menial work (low-value, low uniqueness). This concept in turn links in to the earlier discussion around internal labour markers and firm-specific skills.

However, in practice (a criticism that is equally applied to the flexible firm model) it can be difficult to define what skill sets are actually conducive to externalization. To paraphrase Purcell *et al.* (2004), pure conditions favouring externalization, as extrapolated from theory rarely exist. Even low-skilled work can require social interdependency, as seen in team-working and other instances of organization-specific knowledge of clients, products and processes (*ibid.*).

Moreover, even if firms display strategic intent, they might not have the capabilities to truly implement HRM in a strategic manner. Cappelli and Keller (2014) argue that the incidence of strategic, or at least co-ordinated HR activity, seems to have decreased in recent decades, if US evidence is indicative. Citing NICB and Janger (1966) they comment that in the mid-1960s, 96 per cent of "personnel departments" conducted some type of workforce planning; whereas by the mid-1990s, comparable surveys suggested that only 19 per cent of companies stated that they engaged in any form of "structured workforce planning". This atrophy of strategic intent by US firms was also evident in a comparable decline in the incidence of firms undertaking succession planning (*ibid.*: 313). In one sense, given the erosion of internal labour market structures and more volatile market environments, this should not be surprising – but it does question the notion that firms have become more strategic as a result of the pressures brought about in the era of globalization.

In addition, management-centric models that posit strategic intent ignore the ability of workers themselves to shape labour use practices (Rubery 1978; Grimshaw & Rubery 1998). As such, the growth of flexible forms of work might not reflect employer intent per se, but rather be an outcome of supply-side constraints – particularly where certain types of worker are in short supply. Hence, workers with key skills could take account of their market power and seek to go to the external market themselves (Albert & Bradley 1998; Harvey & Kanwall 2000; Kunda *et al.* 2002), as "free agents". Alternatively, workers might decide to go to the external market not for the attraction of being a free agent, but rather, to escape the erosion of working conditions or bureaucracy attached to a permanent job (Grimshaw *et al.* 2003; Purcell *et al.* 2004; De Ruyter *et al.* 2008).

Not that this has stopped firms seeking to segment their workforce according to whom is actually vital to the running of their business, and tailoring HR policies and practices accordingly. It is notable that in the 20 years or so since Lepak and Snell wrote their highly influential piece, the discourse on labour market segmentation has in effect been turned on its head, with the emergence of more prescriptive literature on "talent management". Indeed, this has been pioneered notably by segmentation theorists such as Peter Cappelli in the US, mentioned earlier. Thus the earlier literature on how firms operating within a given sector might structure their workforces has been replaced by something rather more instrumental, in terms of how firms *should* structure their workforce (despite a barrage of criticism of Atkinson's more ambiguous earlier work in this vein). Cappelli (2008) is notable in this regard in terms of his argument, although he is at pains to point out that in a volatile market environment, "talent management" should not be conflated with long-term workforce/succession planning but, rather, adaptability in accordance with supply chain management tenets (i.e., "talent on demand"; *ibid.*: 7).

Of course, such talent management approaches can only be effectively conducted with cognizance of the worker's individual work–life trajectory and consequent *psychological contract* (Rousseau 1995; Coyle-Shapiro & Kessler 2000) upon entering a work environment.[7] As noted above, this is of particular resonance to those workers that aspire to "escape" a rigid organizational environment because their implicit expectations are antithetical to being subordinate to an imposed bureaucracy/organizational hierarchy.

These are the arguments that have been put forward by proponents of

---

7. Violations of the psychological contract (i.e., the implicit set of expectations that workers bring into an employment relationship) were typically found to result in reduced levels of commitment and "organizational citizenship" behaviour (Coyle-Shapiro & Kessler 2000).

the gig economy. Carson (2012, cited in Friedman 2015: 173) claims that gig work enables full-time employees to do self-employment "on the side" – to test the waters before shedding employee status, as it were. At one level this might be seen as desirable by workers who seek to forego job security and shed the ties of commitment to an organization and the necessary accommodation of operating in a bureaucratic, hierarchical structure. In this sense, terms such as "flexible" or "gig" can infer that fluid, competitive labour markets are "good". As Geoff Nunberg notes, the term gig "strikes just the right jaunty, carefree note", somehow fitting, amidst a dominant capitalist ideological context of rampant individualism and short time horizons.[8] In contrast, terms such as "precarious" or "contingent" infer that such markets are somehow necessarily "bad".

Significantly, the above discussion implies that the notion that "talent management" may in itself be contingent as to the expectancy of significant tenure within any one organization. As Standing's (1997) discussion on "proficians" and Cappelli's (2008) caveat around a volatile market environment make clear, the implications are that "talented" workers can (and do, or otherwise "have to") make frequent recourse to the external labour market. However, the popular conception of the gig economy is that it is more typified by highly commodified labour with low wages and low skill sets that are by definition the very antithesis of "talent". Hence, such competing views of the appeal, efficiency and welfare-generating properties of flexible labour markets necessitate a detailed examination of gig work arrangements across countries, so as to critically evaluate the claims that workers "choose" to enter such arrangements.

Summary

This chapter has provided an overview of various theoretical perspectives pertaining to labour market flexibility, so as to provide a conceptual underpinning for working in the gig economy. In so doing we started with the simple neoclassical economics view of flexibility as being epitomized by a perfectly competitive labour market. In moving on from this abstraction

---

8. See http://www.npr.org/2016/01/11/460698077/goodbye-jobs-hello-gigs-nunbergs-word-of-the-year-sums-up-a-new-economic-reality (accessed 15 October 2018).

we then sought to posit an account of how institutional factors have been pivotal in shaping the evolution of labour markets over the course of the twentieth century. These factors were evident with the increasing dominance of large firms that saw distinct advantages in internalizing paid work via permanent full-time employment; and accompanying socio-political factors that reinforced these tendencies in industrialized economies with the post-Second World War establishment of the welfare state.

In so doing, what becomes evident is that regardless of theoretical arguments as to the efficiency of competitive markets (or otherwise), the actual nature of labour flexibility in an economy will be dictated by the changing parameters of the power relations between capital and labour in an economy. In this context, the emergence of internal labour markets was driven by the increased power of labour in the 25 years after the Second World War (and the existence of communism, which gave would-be agitators against capitalism something else to gravitate to if their demands were ignored or suppressed by the state). More recently (over the last 30 years or so), the internationalization of production has served to increase labour supply globally, which has weakened the bargaining power of labour in any individual country. To these developments then, technological change has enabled companies to outsource labour in ways that simply would not have been possible 50 years ago. Conversely, at the high end of the jobs market, it has also led to an increasing emphasis on "talent".

It is thus the context of globalization, market-led re-regulation of the employment relationship, and technological change that has created the conditions underpinning the gig economy (which in turn has led to new forms of labour market segmentation and re-commodification within and across countries). However, there is also a need to distil arguments whether people choose to undertake gig work, or whether it is done simply because regular work is not available. That is, to what extent can its emergence be accounted for by choice-theoretic approaches, as opposed to arguments that posit it in terms of the re-commodification of labour? In the following chapter we explore international trends in forms of work that could be defined as "gig work" and also explore the reasons why people undertake such work.

3

Working in the gig economy: international trends

This chapter builds on the previous discussion that has conceptualized and theorized gig work to explore trends in the gig economy. The first section introduces a discussion on how to operationalize gig work; that is, to define it in terms of categories of work that statistics agencies provide data for – our key postulate here being that there is no distinct statistical measure of gig work, and that a number of types of work share its features. Hence, we operationalize gig work in terms of four highly contingent types of employment: casual work, temporary agency work, zero-hours contracts, and dependent contractors.

The following sections then examine trends in these forms of work and provide a critical analysis of the factors that have driven their growth or resurgence. In so doing, what is notable is that despite widespread claims that gig work will become the "new norm", empirical evidence suggests that the four forms of work identified still remain as relatively minor components of the workforce in developed countries. However, this is not to downplay the significance of gig work, but rather we argue that the impact of gig work on the economy is not in its direct incidence, but rather the potential impact that such forms of work can have on employment elsewhere.

Operationalizing gig work

In attempting to understand trends in gig work, it is first necessary to operationalize gig work in terms of work and employment categories that national and international statistical agencies would utilize. As such, gig work has been seen as most coterminous with the status of being a dependent contractor, in being available on-demand and generally working through one organization (as demonstrated by Uber). A narrower definition of gig work would be to specify contractors or freelancers that are sourced via the intermediary of an online platform, which is where the novelty of the gig economy as a term largely originated. This is the definition cited by De Stefano (2016), who denotes work in the gig economy as constituting both "crowd-work" (that is, where a number of firms and workers are connected via an online platform) and "on-demand work", whereby a single user firm uses an online platform to match workers to demand for services.

There has been significant growth in the number of such platform operators in recent years, as De Stefano attests, with firms such as Uber and Amazon now widely-recognized global household names. The operation of such firms is truly international, although more notably present in liberal market economies such as the United States and the UK. The website Casual Capitalist[9] purports that the "top ten" online platforms in the US are: Uber (taxi services), Lyft (another on-line platform competing with Uber for driver services), Turo (a platform for renting out one's vehicle to travellers), Airbnb (a room rental service), Postmates (a delivery service), Instacart (a grocery delivery service), Taskrabbit (a platform for tradesperson services), Freelancer (a professional service for areas such as publishing, design, marketing, etc.), Upwork (professional services such as software development and graphic design), and WeGoLook (an inspection service for buyers looking to vet purchases made online).

The profit margins associated with such providers are also significant – Aloisi (2016) suggests that "the on-line platforms retain for themselves, on average, 15% of the fee, and exclude all liabilities" (*ibid.*: 665). Turning to workforce estimates for the gig economy, Smith and Seberstein (2015; cited in De Stefano 2016) suggest that the size of the workforce for the largest platform/online app/crowd-work providers such as Care.com and Crowdsource runs into the millions. These figures are reproduced in Table 3.1. Other estimates, reflecting more of a consensus, suggest that stereotypical gig work as mediated through online platforms is relatively insignificant – typically at less than 1 per cent of the workforce (Stewart & Stanford 2017). Stewart and Stanford (*ibid.*) provide a useful synopsis here, for example citing Farrell and Greig (2016), who estimated that only 0.4 per cent of New York residents used an online labour platform during any given month in 2015 and 0.6

---

9. See https://thecasualcapitalist.com/the-sharing-economy/gig-economy-platforms-top-ten/ (accessed 9 February 2018).

per cent a capital platform. The Bureau of Labor Statistics (BLS) (2018a), in their contingent and alternative employment arrangements supplement, have recently released calculations (from 30 September 2018) on "electronically mediated employment" and found that such workers in the US as at May 2017 only accounted for about 1 per cent of the workforce.[10] Katz and Krueger (2016) cited Huws and Joyce (2016a, 2016b) who conducted online surveys in the UK, Germany and Sweden and estimated that 3–4 per cent of workers utilized online platforms in any month; and citing Minifie (2016), who estimated that only 80,000 Australians (less than 0.5% of the workforce) regularly did work via a digital platform. However, as Aloisi (2016: 659) reminds us, attempts to quantify the size of the gig economy workforce are further compromised by the fact that there "is no distinction between active and inactive accounts … and a worker – in the absence of an exclusivity clause – could sign up to several platforms" (*ibid.*).

However, confining discussion of trends in gig work solely to that of trends in dependent contracting facilitated via an online platform would be

Table 3.1 Major online platform and app companies' workforce, estimates

Name	Sector	Size of workforce	Country operations
Uber	Transportation	160,000	International
Lyft	Transportation	50,000	US
Sidecar	Transportation	6,000	Major US cities
Handy	Home services	5,000	US
Taskrabbit	Home services	30,000	International
Care.com	Home Services	6,600,000	International
Postmates	Delivery	10,000	US
Amazon Mechanical Turk	Crowdwork	500,000	International
Crowdflower	Crowdwork	5,000,000	International
Crowdsource	Crowdwork	8,000,000	International
Clickworker	Crowdwork	700,000	International

Source: Smith & Leberstein 2015, cited in De Stefano 2016.

---

10. Wider measures of "related forms" of work reveal that "[i]n May 2017, there were 10.6 million independent contractors (6.9 percent of total employment), 2.6 million on-call workers (1.7 percent of total employment), 1.4 million temporary help agency workers (0.9 percent of total employment), and 933,000 workers provided by contract firms (0.6 percent of total employment)" (BLS 2018b).

limiting and problematic for two reasons. The first is that labour force surveys tend to ask respondents to self-identify with categories of employment in their *main* job, but do not ask how their labour supply is matched to labour demand as it were, so it would be problematic to identify such workers using aggregate data. And to reiterate Aloisi's (2016) point, a preoccupation with main job status also excludes multiple job-holders, which could potentially underestimate the extent of gig work. The second is because matching labour supply to labour demand via online platforms is also a feature of other flexible, on-demand forms of work such as casual employment and agency work. Indeed, as Stanford (2017: 285) notes, such digital intermediation could equally apply to electronic rostering systems, and web-based monitoring and communications systems. None of these are necessarily incompatible with more "conventional" forms of employment. Therefore, in trying to understand the trends in gig working, a broader definition is needed, one based on exploring trends in those forms of work characterized by workers essentially being available on-demand, which is not solely the preserve of dependent contractors.

In doing this we also seek to link gig work to wider debates on precarious work, where labour market and socio-economic context is all-important. For example, secondary school students working in marginal part-time jobs, could be said to engage in a precarious form of work; but their own work–life trajectory is not necessarily precarious (and subjectively, nor would they necessarily perceive it as such; Campbell & Price 2016). Hence, one also needs to draw a distinction between working voluntarily in the gig economy, and those who take gig work because they are unable to obtain a regular (permanent) job. In the discussion that follows, we identify four such categories: dependent contractors, casual employees/workers, agency employees/workers, and zero-hours contract employees/workers. These forms of work can be considered as highly commodified in that all the risks associated with any loss of income due to work being unavailable are associated with the worker (Rubery & Grimshaw 2015) – a key feature of the gig economy.

In considering this, the caveat that national data sources can vary in terms of how employment categories are defined must also be borne in mind. As such, it is possible that some conflation of employment categories can occur, such as equating "casual" employment with "temporary" employment, which includes fixed-term contract work and temporary agency work as well as casual/seasonal work. In this context, the International Labour Organization (ILO) (2016: 21) provide a useful diagram of the different forms of non-standard/flexible work to highlight the overlapping nature of the many forms of such work. They argue that temporary agency work, for example, overlaps with fixed-term contract work, because in many countries, "this is the legal form that an employment relationship between an agency and a worker can take" (*ibid.*). In India, it is evident that the vast majority of own-account workers (i.e. self-employed) are also temporary contract workers and therefore in essence dependent contractors (ILO 2018a/b).

For EU countries a degree of harmonization of definitions is possible because of the existence of Eurostat data such as that in the European Labour Force Survey (ELFS), but elsewhere organizations such as the ILO tend to rely on national statistics agencies, and so "[t]here are wide differences in definitions used across countries, which should be kept in mind when making cross-country comparisons" (ILO 2018a). The incidence of multiple job-holding (ILO 2016) also needs to be considered in assessing the extent of these forms of work as it is likely that those engaged in part-time and temporary work would need to engage in more than one job to attain a sustainable income. Indeed, ILO estimates for multiple job-holders suggest that it is a significant phenomenon in the workforce, with 4–6 per cent of workers in developed countries, and 20–30 per cent of workers in developing countries, engaged in multiple jobs (*ibid.*: 197). A final caveat in terms of estimating the incidence of different forms of work is that statistics from developing or emerging economy countries in particular should be treated with caution. The trends in temporary contract work – that is, work whereby "workers are engaged only for a specific period of time, includes fixed-term, project- or task-based contracts, as well as seasonal or casual work, including day labour" (ILO 2018a) are depicted in Figure 3.1.

Evident from Table 3.2 is that the proportion of temporary contract work over the period in question has remained relatively stable across countries for the past ten years, with only Spain demonstrating a marked downturn (off a very high base) during the recessionary period, 2007–09. The Russian Federation and India also show downturns after 2009, but in other countries such as France and Canada the overall incidence of temporary work held steady, or continued to grow, during the economic downturn. This suggests that simple explanations of temporary contracts as being correlated to the

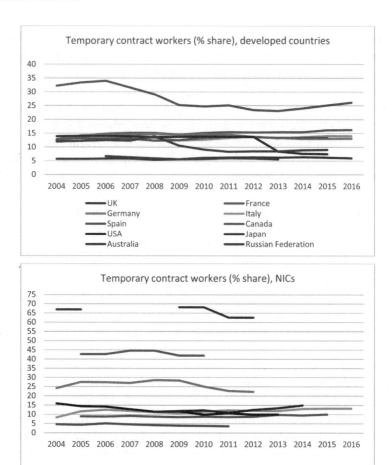

Figure 3.1 Temporary contract workers (% share), selected developed and NIC economies, 2005–17

Source: ILO 2018a.

Note: As this data is based on national definitions, some caution should be used in making comparisons. For example, whilst the ILO include casual employment under the label of "temporary contract", the definition of "casual employment" in Australia is based upon lack of entitlement to standard employment benefits, not tenure of contract (ILO 2016). The figures above for Australia then do not capture casual work in the Australian context, for which according to the Australian definition comprises about one quarter of the workforce (see discussion on casual work below).

business cycle (either directly or inversely) are insufficient. Given the heterogeneous nature of temporary work, it is evident that factors will differ across countries and between industries, a complete exposition of which is beyond the scope of this book (as with fixed-term contract employment, for example).

We explore further the reasons for trends in temporary contracts by considering casual employment and temporary agency work; two forms of work that share many features of gig economy work. However, it is worth noting at this stage to what extent temporary contract work is seen as the outcome of individual choice, that is, the reasons why people work on a limited-duration basis. Data for this is available from the European Labour Force Survey, and is reproduced in Table 3.2.

Table 3.2 Reasons given for working on a fixed-term basis, EU countries, 2014 (%)

Reason given	Men	Women	Total
Could not find a permanent job	61.6	63.2	62.3
Undergoing school education or training	18.1	16.7	17.5
Did not want a permanent job	11.1	11.9	11.5
Held a probationary contract	9.1	8.2	8.7
Total	100	100	100

Source: reproduced from ILO 2016: 58.

It is notable from Table 3.2 that a majority of workers on fixed-term contracts in the EU during 2014 were doing so because they could not obtain a permanent job, and that there were no noticeable gender effects in this finding. A breakdown by country, however, shows some variation in this, ranging from about 10 per cent in Austria, to over 85 per cent in Spain, Romania and Cyprus during 2014 (*ibid.*).

Casual employment

Casual employment is a form of temporary contract employment, which is typically defined as that whereby the employee works for a limited duration and is paid by the number of hours worked in a given period. It thus typically differs from permanent employment, in that notice can be given immediately, rather than with a specified minimum period, and each engagement of casual work could therefore be regarded as a separate contract of employment (Brooks 1985). A common international legal definition of casual employment, however, is lacking. Nevertheless, the key characteristics of casual work are those of contingency and flexibility of work patterns, and it is these characteristics that generally define it under national labour laws (ILO 2016: 23). Some countries (e.g., Australia) highlight the lack of entitlement to certain employment benefits such as annual leave, in determining casual status. In this sense, work is deemed as casual not because of being of limited duration with variable hours, but by exclusion from some, or all, aspects of the framework of protective employment regulation. This is particularly so for the somewhat oxymoronic category denoted as "regular casuals", i.e., those with continuous tenure in their current job for at least a year, which belies public perceptions of such work.

In Australia, for example, the incidence of casual employment increased dramatically in the 1980s and 1990s as businesses embraced opportunities opened up by labour market and product market deregulation, combined with an increase in labour market participation by groups such as students and females. The UK's relatively low level of temporary contract work is often argued to be the case because of its relatively flexible laws on hiring and firing meaning that businesses do not seek the same recourse to use temporary contracts to get around labour market rigidities (Rubery & Grimshaw 2015). In Australia, however, the incidence of "casual" employees (those without paid leave entitlements) was estimated in August 2017 at 25.1 per cent of the workforce (and of these, 69% were "full-time" and 31% were "part-time") (ABS 2017) – in a labour market with a similar level of regulation to that of the UK.

This suggests that the relationship between national labour law frameworks and the extent of contingent forms of work is more complex. Other institutional, structural and sectoral factors also need to be taken into account, particularly in service sector occupations (Jaehrling & Méhout 2012). In Australia, casual employment is most prevalent in the retail, hospitality and agricultural sectors (all sectors with minimal to non-existent union representation), although it grew across all industries as a form of employment during the 1980s and 1990s, and has since maintained a more-or-less constant share of the workforce (ILO 2016: 65). The wide extent of such work in a relatively deregulated labour market environment suggests that employers are not utilizing these workers to avoid employment protection laws, in other words because they *need* to, but rather because they *want* to.

The Australian phenomenon of casual employment being a structural feature of one-quarter of the workforce for the past 20 years is somewhat unique for a developed country. The incidence of casual work and seasonal work is far lower in other developed countries, for example, Canada, where each has steadily remained at a level of approximately 3 per cent of total waged employment over the period 1997–2014 (ILO 2016: 64). In the United States, some 2.1 per cent of employees were "direct hire" temporary employees (a term loosely synonymous with casual work) during 2005, reflecting the low level of temporary work overall (*ibid.*).

Casual employment as a distinct form of work characterized by lack of employment benefits and being paid an hourly rate is a feature more symptomatic of the labour markets of developing countries and emerging economies. In Pakistan, it comprised 42 per cent of total waged employment, whilst in India and Bangladesh (as the predominant form of temporary contract) it comprised some two-thirds of total employment (most recent data available cited in ILO 2016: 68). Traditionally, casual employment in newly industrialized countries (NICs) was typically found in agriculture, but in the last 15 years as global supply chains have expanded into these countries, sectoral shifts in employment have occurred and labour market regulations have been loosened (ILO 2016), it has grown in other sectors, such as manufacturing. In Pakistan, casual employment comprised approximately 70 per cent of employment in manufacturing during 2009, whilst in Indonesia its share increased to 25 per cent of employment in manufacturing by 2012 (ILO 2016: 69).

Temporary agency work

Temporary agency work constitutes a heterogeneous category of activity that includes working for outplacement agencies, contract labour agencies and agencies for the recruitment and placement of foreign workers. The distinguishing feature of agency work in most countries, as opposed to a regular employment relationship, is that the temporary agency worker (TAW), the temporary work agency (TWA) and the user enterprise are linked together by a triangular relationship containing two different types of contract: a contract of employment between the agency worker and the TWA; and a job assignment contract between the TWA and the user enterprise (ILO 1994: 15). Hence, the agency worker would be legally employed by the TWA, and the user enterprise would be responsible for on-site issues such as job supervision and health and safety at work (*ibid.*). The employee status of agency workers has not always been clear, however (Caire 1989: 104), and in actuality depends upon the particular legislation found in individual countries. The issue of regulation is one we return to in following sections.

Industry data for the extent of temporary agency work is provided by the global peak body for the sector, the World Employment Confederation (previously the CIETT, i.e., the International Confederation of Private Employment Services),[11] which promotes itself as "[e]nabling work, adaptation, security & prosperity" (WEC 2018: 6). The explicit implication here is that TAW has a positive economic and societal role to play in well-functioning labour markets. This is a theme we consider more critically later in assessing reasons for the use of TAW. As an industry in itself, providing labour hire and recruitment services for organizations, the sector has displayed considerable growth across countries. The WEC state that their affiliates comprise over 169,000 TWA/recruitment companies, directly employing over 1.5 million individuals to "help people navigate the labour market" and a headcount of approximately 43 million agency workers (*ibid.*: 9–10). Utilizing the WEC figures, Table 3.3 illustrates the number of TAWs for the estimated top ten countries. Notably this data suggests that TAW is engaged with as extensively in NICs such as China and India, as it is in mature economies.

However, this data should be treated with some caution as the figures provided only pertain to affiliated member companies (that is, this data could understate the actual incidence of TAW). It is also unclear from this data whether any of these individuals hold down an employee position elsewhere (and hence could be "moonlighting"), or are otherwise multiple job-holders; whether with more than one TWA, or a combination of direct employment and agency work (that the data is presented as "headcount" would imply this).

In considering the distribution of TAW, lower-skilled occupations feature more prominently, although not exclusively so: US BLS data from 2012

---

11. See http://www.wecglobal.org/economicreport2016/index.html (accessed 15 October 2018).

Table 3.3 Agency worker (TAW) headcount, top 10 countries, 2017

Country	TAW headcount
United States	15,600,000
China	8,680,000
Japan	2,630,325
India	2,100,000
France	2,000,000
Mexico	1,765,101
UK	1,198,000
Germany	949,227
South Africa	900,000
Poland	799,727
World total	43,319,404

Source: WEC 2018: 10.

suggested that 16.2 per cent of "human resources specialists" and 15.1 per cent of "data entry keyers" in the US were agency workers (cited in ILO 2016: 88). However, most of these workers were found in "production jobs" (43.7%) and "office jobs" (41.2%) – predominantly clerical (*ibid.*). Similar figures were also reported for Canada, with 43 per cent of TAWs being found in "processing jobs" in manufacturing and utilities. The ILO also reported TAW as the most rapidly-growing form of non-standard employment in the European Union during the 1990s (*ibid.*). TAW also appeared to be more prevalent amongst younger workers, if ELFS data is indicative, with 2012 figures suggesting that 2.9 per cent of workers aged 15–24 in selected countries[12] were engaged in TAW, as opposed to 1.3 per cent of those aged 25–54 and only 0.7 per cent of those aged 55–64. For younger workers, TAW might have had an innate appeal in that it could readily be combined with studying, as reported with students who did not want a permanent job (cited in ILO 2016: 136).

Turning to trends in TAW, the ILO (2016: 87) argue that agency work grew "rapidly" in the 1990s across the world, with for example, the percentage of TAW in the US workforce doubling between 1990 and 2000 (*ibid.*). In Japan, the incidence of TAW (known as "dispatched workers" in

---

12. These countries were: Belgium, Estonia, France, Germany, Greece, Hungary, Ireland, Italy, Netherlands, Poland, Portugal, Spain, Sweden and the UK.

the local jargon) increased from 0.5 per cent of the workforce during 1999 to 2.1 per cent during 2015 (ILO 2016: 92). The European Foundation for the Improvement of Living and Working Conditions, via their *Conditions of Work Survey*, also attempts to assess the incidence of temporary agency work over time, although this is limited to European countries. Data for these countries is presented in Figure 3.2 (unsurprisingly, given that they would corroborate to full-time equivalent (FTE), they equate to a lower incidence of TAW than that implied by WEC headcount figures). Whilst generalizations about trends in TAW are problematic due to a lack of comparable data, the existence of European data (European Labour Force Survey, or ELFS) does enable a modicum of comparison between 28 countries and hence enable some inferences to be drawn about trends in agency work and driving factors.

Examining the incidence of TAW over time in the countries depicted in Figure 3.2, however, suggests that it is problematic to simply explain this as being due to cyclical factors related to the state of the economy. On the one hand, it is possible to argue that the incidence of TAW (as with other forms of non-standard employment) should be inversely related to the business

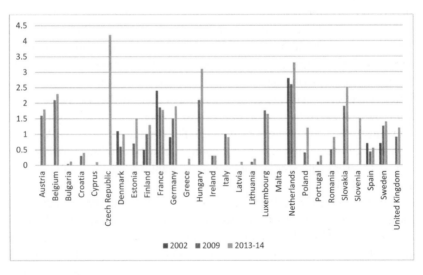

Source: EurWORK 2009, 2016

Figure 3.2 Temporary agency work (% share) in EU-28 selected countries, 2002–14

cycle: rising during an economic downturn, as employers' bargaining power increases and hence with less need to hire permanent employees; but falling as the economy improves and employers need to take on more permanent employees as worker bargaining power increases (Bosch 2004: 630). On the other hand, it could equally be argued that TAW provides a flexible buffer during an economic downturn, and hence, the number of TAWs should fall as the economy worsens, as employers let go of such peripheral workers first. Indeed, such arguments would accord with the postulates of models such as Atkinson's "flexible firm" discussed in Chapter 2. There is some evidence to support this, with TAW comprising a disproportionate 26 per cent of net job losses during the 2001 recession in the US, and 10.6 per cent of net job losses in the US during the 2008–09 recession (ILO 2016: 87).

However, even given the limitations of the data in Figure 3.2 (with data not available for all countries in each year), it is evident that TAW trends across countries do not conform to simple cyclical explanations. In some countries (e.g., France, Netherlands, Spain), the incidence of TAW fell after the economic downturn in 2007–08, lending some credence to the flexible buffer view of their function in the labour market. However, in other countries (e.g., Germany, Hungary, Sweden), the incidence of TAW increased during the recessionary period, and continued to increase into the recovery phase after 2010, perhaps lending credence to the notion that employers in these countries increasingly see TAW as an alternative to standard employment arrangements. For Grimshaw and Rubery (2015: 240) this would vindicate their position that non-standard employment (of which TAW is one example) is not a "protective buffer" for standard employment, but rather has increasingly provided "a competitive challenge to terms and conditions within standard contracts" (a theme we return to later).

Other explanations for the use of TAW point to supply-side developments, particularly in the public sector and/or with more skilled workers (echoing the mention of "freelancers" earlier) – a debate which is usually linked to the existence of skills shortages in key professions such as teachers and nurses. Here, the effect of government funding cuts and recruitment freezes to permanent posts during an economic downturn is argued to create conditions favourable to the increased use of TAW (Kirkpatrick *et al.* 2011). Alternatively, workers such as nurses and social workers could see "temping" as a means of "escape" from what they perceive as increased bureaucracy and managerialism, thereby allowing them to pick and choose work assignments and avoid the strictures of operating in an organizational hierarchy (De Ruyter *et al.* 2008). Such individuals have been referred to in the literature as "free agents" (Pink 2001) and could take advantage of their labour market power to secure considerable premiums as contingent workers over that of permanent employment (Kunda *et al.* 2002).

The above notwithstanding, it should be noted that despite a considerable body of literature being devoted to the "growth" of TAW, it is striking that it still exists only as a relatively small element of the workforce in most countries. The EuroFound data presented suggests that the Czech Republic displayed the highest incidence of TAW in the EU-28 in 2013–14, at just over 4 per cent of employment.

On-call work and zero-hours contract employees

Zero-hours contract employees are defined as workers whose contract of employment requires them to be available on demand, but with no guarantee of any fixed hours of work (Brinkley 2013). These workers effectively come under the label of "marginal part time employment" (ILO 2016: 27). That such workers "have to be available as and when their employer needs them" (Brinkley 2013: 7) also effectively prohibits them as part of their contract to work for any other employer during its length of operation. Even if this is not the case, the UK industrial relations body ACAS (2014; cited in Rubery & Grimshaw 2015: 246) suggested that some workers feared that if they expressed unavailability for a shift, then they would be "excluded" from future work. Such workers pose a problem for conventional definitions of employment, as depending on when they are asked in labour force surveys, they could, for example, variously be hidden under "self-employment", "part-time employment" or "casual employment".

What data there is suggests that zero-hours contract work in some countries has grown significantly since the 2008 downturn. In the UK, work by John Philpott for the Resolution Foundation estimated that some 2.9 per cent of the workforce were on a zero-hours contracts during 2016 (*The Guardian*, 15 November 2016)[13], having increased from 0.5 per cent in 2006.

---

13. See https://www.theguardian.com/uk-news/2016/nov/15/more-than-7m-britons-in-precarious-employment (accessed 27 May 2018).

Analysis of this data by occupation suggested that zero-hours contracts were most prevalent in "elementary occupations" (approximately 10% of employees) and "caring, leisure and other service occupations" (approximately 7% of employees), although such contracts could also be found amongst higher-skilled occupations, such as managers (*ibid.*). However, there is some evidence to suggest that the growth of zero-hours contracts might have ebbed, with the impending impact of Brexit possibly acting to reduce the supply of workers willing to work for uncertain hours (Monaghan 2017). The Resolution Foundation reported that the "zero-hours juggernaut may have come to a halt", with the rate of growth abating noticeably during the second half of 2016; from 7.7 per cent at the same time in 2015, to only 0.8 per cent (*ibid.*). Approximately 10 per cent of the US workforce had "irregular and on-call work schedules", with the lowest income workers more likely to report these types of work arrangements (ILO 2016: xxiii.), whilst a 2010 survey suggested that 3.5 per cent of US employees were on-call workers (day labourers), having increased from 2.5 per cent during 2005 (*ibid.*: 63).

Estimates for "mini jobs" in Germany (a similar concept to zero-hours contracts) suggest that the use of these contracts is particularly prevalent in jobs such as cleaning (including public-sector bodies such as hospitals) and sales assistants (Jaehrling & Méhout 2012). The use of mini jobs in these sectors (often via outsourcing) had enabled employers to largely avoid social insurance contributions or works council censure (*ibid.*). Until 2013, reduced social security contributions were a key characteristic of such marginal part-time work, with a threshold of €400 (ILO 2016: 162). Hence, it is not surprising that the incidence of mini jobs in Germany had increased significantly, from 5.6 per cent of total employment during 2003, to 7.7 per cent during 2015 (cited in ILO 2016: 162). In Poland, the use of "commercial contracts" by employers has become increasingly prominent, with approximately 10 per cent of the working population utilized on such a basis in 2012, fomenting concerns from the country's Labour Inspectorate that such workers often should be on regular employment contracts (*ibid.*: 57).

The growth of zero-hours contracts in particular sectors, such as the services provided by Deliveroo (a take-away meal courier delivery service), does suggest that regulatory factors could be a key reason for the increase in jobs clearly associated with the "gig economy". Deliveroo's workforce in the UK in 2016 consisted of what the company described as some 8,000 "independent suppliers" (*The Guardian*, 15 November 2016). However, in the

Netherlands and Germany its workforce consisted of approximately 1,500 persons directly employed by the company (*ibid.*). This throws into relief how the same occupation can be subject to very different terms and conditions of work depending on the nature of the regulatory framework (or lack thereof), a theme we take up further in Chapter 4.

Dependent contractors

Dependent contractors, otherwise known under the category of "dependent self-employment" (ILO 2016: 98), are defined by being self-employed, but only having one customer, or at most, a few, and moreover, that they have no autonomy in so far as they "receive detailed instructions in how the work is to be done" (*ibid.*). In a number of cases, such workers might previously have been employees of enterprises which they now serve as (outsourced) dependent contractors, with all the attendant costs, risks and responsibilities transferred onto them (Mühlberger 2007; cited by Thörnquist 2015: 412).[14] In this sense, one of the key characteristics of the gig economy that being a dependent contractor epitomizes, as opposed to conventional forms of employment, is that the worker "owns" most, or all, of the means of production (Stewart & Stanford 2017), be it a motorbike for Deliveroo deliveries, or a car for Uber drivers.

Whilst it should not be surmized that all gig economy work is necessarily coterminous with the status of being a dependent contractor, it is evident that the on-demand nature of the work (in common with casual workers, zero-hours contract workers and temporary agency workers) does not lend itself readily to gig economy workers being multiple-job holders, or in other words dealing with more than one client. It is therefore in respect to these workers that much of the concern around the growth of gig work has centred.

Unfortunately obtaining data on growth trends in such forms of work is difficult to obtain, and one is largely reliant on supplementary questions in national labour force surveys (ILO 2016). The ILO note that even countries such as Spain and Germany "do not explicitly address this employment

---

14. Such work is also the preserve of groups already vulnerable in society, such as migrant workers, and links into the related debate on the "grey area" of the labour market (Thörnquist 2015).

category in their labour force surveys" (*ibid*.: 98). An exception is Italy, which identifies a category of worker labelled as "para-subordinates" (or, "*collaboratori*"). The ILO (*ibid*.) cited that such workers comprised 1.7 per cent of total employment in Italy during 2014. Evidence from the European Working Conditions Survey 2010 suggested that dependent contractors as a percentage of the non-agricultural private sector workforce in European countries varied from "negligible" in Sweden to over 3 per cent in the Czech Republic, Greece, Italy and Slovakia (*ibid*.: 99). In Australia, estimates suggested that dependent contractors comprised 1.7 per cent of total employment during 2013 (*ibid*.: 100), whilst in Mexico, "subordinated workers who did not receive a wage" comprised over 4 per cent of employment during 2014 (*ibid*.).

However, dependent contractors are a subset of workers known as "own-account workers", that is, self-employed workers who have no employees of their own. Data on own-account workers are plentiful. Historically, at least, such work has for the most part, been a feature of developing countries (ILO 2016) and one would have expected its incidence to drop as a country becomes more developed and the formal sector comprising waged employment increases. Accordingly, Figure 3.3 outlines trends in own-account working for selected (key) developed and NIC economies. From this, two things should be noted. First, the incidence of own-account work in NIC economies is generally showing a static, or downward trend (with the notable exception of India, as mentioned earlier, where there seems to be significant overlap between this form of work and that denoted as temporary contract work). Second, of all countries depicted, the UK situation appears almost unique in showing a manifest increase in the incidence of this form of work, increasing from 9.7 per cent in 2005 to 12.6 per cent in 2016.

The UK situation is worth exploring further, as there is evidence to suggest that the growth of this form of work can be linked to government policies of pushing the unemployed into contingent forms of employment (including self-employment) after 2010, most notably under the introduction of Universal Credit (UC) as a replacement for Job Seeker's Allowance, as the strictures on UC did not involve capping work at 16 hours per week in order to maintain benefit entitlement (Cain 2016). In this context, Cain noted that the premise of UC was to specifically adapt the unemployment benefits regime to "'flexible work patterns' convenient to modern employers" – usually through the use of zero-hours contracts (*ibid*.: 490). In this context,

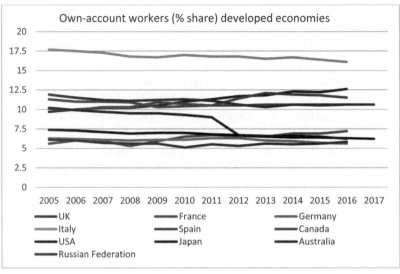

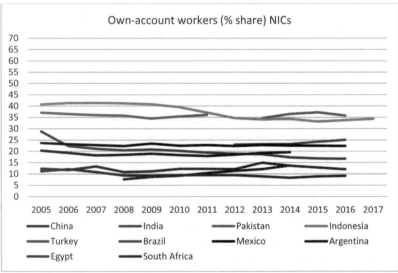

Figure 3.3 Own-account workers (% share), selected developed and NIC economies, 2005–17

Source: ILO 2018b.

Note: The figures for the USA and China should be treated with caution, as they include employers.

there is evidence to suggest that total employment growth in the UK in the aftermath of the 2008–09 recession could almost be entirely accounted for by the growth in self-employment, as the net number of employee jobs in the UK economy did not increase again until 2014, whereas the incidence of self-employment continued to increase during and after the recession (ONS 2018).

Of course, promoting and utilizing flexible or marginal forms of work as a means to reduce unemployment is nothing new. Indeed, various legislative initiatives to liberalize or subsidize the use of temporary contracts were a feature of European economies during the 1990s and 2000s on the purported justification of opening up overly-rigid labour markets (Siebert 1997; Gerfin et al. 2005). These initiatives were notably espoused under the auspices of the 1994 OECD Jobs Strategy (Casey 2004) and the 1997 European Employment Strategy (in execution, if not intent; Raveaud 2007). However, in contrast to more regulated continental European economies, the UK context is distinct as it appears to be taking place in an economy that by most measures, already displays a high degree of labour flexibility.

Summary: operationalizing the "significance" of gig economy work

The data presented in this chapter indicates that despite statements of gig economy work having rapidly increased across countries in recent years, actual trends in forms of work that could manifestly be said to be part of the gig economy suggest that gig work remains a relatively minor component of the workforce in developed countries. This is because the form of work that most closely represents that of gig workers, that of the dependent contractor as a subset of own-account workers, remains a minor component of employment in developed countries. Only in the UK, where there is some evidence of a significant increase in the number of own-account workers (and zero-hours contract workers) since the 2008–09 economic downturn, could the phenomenon of gig working be said to have displayed significant growth. In this context, despite the claims of gig working as being a key structural development of capitalist economies, such work could be seen more in the traditional guise of self-employment – rising during an economic downturn as workers are forced into more marginal activities or take on second jobs to maintain an income.

That is not to reduce the significance of gig working as an emergent feature of contemporary capitalist economies. Indeed, the real impact of such forms of work on the labour market is not necessarily in the incidence of them being widely extant. Rather, it is in their impact on eroding the terms and conditions found in more traditional forms of work, i.e., to "gig-ize" the nature of work, so that firms would be more cost-competitive against competitors that utilize such online platforms to reduce their costs. In this sense, we reiterate our point at the start of this chapter in defining gig work; that the use of online platforms to mediate supply and demand is not necessarily unique to the gig economy. This was not lost on Jason Moyer-Lee, general secretary of the Independent Workers Union of Great Britain (IWGB), in an interview with Owen Jones from *The Guardian*: "You can see how the model could be expanded, to coffee chains, or clothing stores". In the same vein, trade unionist Mags Dewhurst commented that "[y]ou could log into a Topshop app, and then join a queue to work" (*ibid.*). Jones further notes that: "[i]t is an attractive proposition for companies, stripping out labour costs and HR. Consider that zero-hours contracts were an obscure innovation until they were rolled out across the economy. It could indeed be a Black Mirror episode. It isn't: it is Britain in 2018. Black Mirror in real time" (*The Guardian*, 24 May 2018).

This chapter thus highlights a need for new measures across countries to capture the actual incidence of platform work (gig work/electronically mediated work). However, with the exception of the recently introduced measure on electronically-mediated modes of work from the US Bureau of Labor Statistics (BLS) mentioned earlier, these are lacking. What is particularly needed is to cross-tabulate a measure of platform work with other indicators such as mode of contract of employment (self-employed, casual employee, etc.), to see to what extent online platform matching of labour supply and demand has become a feature of more traditional forms of employment. In addition, more emphasis needs to be given by statistical agencies to the production of longitudinal data with cohorts of individuals that actually can capture labour market experience over time (as traditional labour force surveys question people at discrete interviews, typically quarterly), if the job churn that characterizes highly precarious forms of work such as gig work is to be captured.

The caveat on the actual incidence of zero-hours contracts in the UK, for example notwithstanding, the potential for "gigification" (Miller 2015) of the labour market could be regarded as the twenty-first century version of the "casualization" of the workforce, as it were. For Grimshaw and Rubery (2015: 240), this is evidence that employers, even in a relatively lightly regulated country such as the UK, are "revealing an appetite for further undermining employment and social protection by using insecure and commodified employment contracts". Or as Aloisi (2016: 662, citing Eyal-Peer *et al.* 2015), puts it: the "sharing economy" has not "introduce[d] the serpent of casual labour into the garden of full employment: it is exploiting an already casualized workforce in ways that will ameliorate some problems as they aggravate others". It is therefore important to consider the attendant terms and conditions of work in the gig economy, and related regulatory issues, in order to draw out wider implications for contemporary workforce developments.

Also evident from the analysis above is that much of what constitutes contingent work is clearly being done on an involuntary basis, that is, that individuals are only engaging in temporary contract work because better alternatives (i.e., obtaining a permanent job) appear to be unavailable. This casts doubts on arguments that seek to explain the emergence of the gig economy purely in terms of choice-theoretic arguments around the preferences being expressed by "free agents". Rather, if such individuals are caught in cycles of precarious work and unemployment (or economic inactivity) then substantive issues arise as to their own well-being. Indeed, one of the key arguments around the economic and societal utility of a standard employment relationship was in its "de-commodification" of labour, so as to enable not only individual well-being, but by providing a modicum of stability for business and wider society, as commented on by Gerhard Bosch:

> Employees are protected from the vagaries of the markets and can make long-term plans for themselves and their families. Firms benefit from a reliable framework within which to plan their work organization and are able to rely on their employees' willingness to cooperate in return for the security they enjoy. In society as a whole, inequalities are reduced and families are able to invest in their members' human capital (Bosch 2004: 621).

Related to debates on the conditions of flexible work forms, Kelliher and Anderson (2010) draw attention to the attendant potential for work intensification. For Kelliher and Anderson, there is an apparent paradox of flexible workers reporting higher job satisfaction and organizational commitment, alongside work intensification. Drawing on their own research study, they suggest that this occurs because employees trade off flexibility for effort – that is, employees respond positively to this by working harder (*ibid.*).

Chapter 4 examines these issues further, with a view to informing the contemporary debate on the actual nature of gig work, so as to critically assess its impact on economic and societal well-being. In so doing, Chapter 4 will critically examine the debate around the gig worker as being an independent contractor, and hence the key debate around such "self-employed" individuals being excluded from the regulatory framework that confers benefits to employees, and why this status differs across countries. Arising from this will then be consideration of how companies in the gig economy respond to the push to extend employment regulation to gig workers (Cherry & Aloisi 2018). This leads to the concluding Chapter 5, which revisits the role of technology as driving developments in the sector; notably, the increased use of automation and artificial intelligence (AI) (Helbing *et al.* 2017). Assessing the veracity of such claims, and considering whether new jobs would be sufficiently created to compensate, is then of the utmost importance.

4

Regulation and the lived experience of
the gig economy

The previous chapter has explored trends in working in the gig economy, by coming up with a classification to operationalize "gig work". In so doing, it was noted that popular claims have been made by commentators of a dramatic increase in such forms of work (to the point of "revolutionizing" production and business operations). However, the actual extent of contingent forms of work coterminous with the gig economy has remained relatively low, if one considers casual work, temporary agency work, zero-hours contracts, and dependent contractors, identified in Chapter 3, as being representative of work in the gig economy. That said, we noted that the significance of the gig economy was not so much in the actual extent of gig work but rather the potential for such a business model to in turn effect (or "gig-ize") other models of business operation, and thus a harbinger of possible future developments.

In this chapter we explore the regulatory framework across countries, as pertains to the terms and conditions surrounding the four forms of work we explored in Chapter 3 (with the caveat that dependent contractors, as a subset of the "self-employed" are predominantly outside of the scope of labour regulations). We then move to examine the debate as to how such regulations operate in practice, so as to provide some objective insights into the "lived experience" faced by workers in the gig economy.

Understanding "regulation"

In Chapter 2 we introduced the simple neoclassical model of the labour market, a so-called "competitive labour market" where the wage was determined solely through the forces of supply and demand and the wage rate that equilibrated the market was referred to as the "market clearing wage". As the competitive labour market is perfectly flexible, any disruptions to supply or demand would quickly result in an adjustment to the wage rate, so that a decreased demand for labour would mean that wages would fall, workers would withdraw from the labour market, and employers could rapidly reduce the size of their workforce or hours worked.

A labour regulation then, in this schema, would be any measure that impedes the free adjustment of supply and demand. Suffice to say, in the simple neoclassical model, any form of regulation would be a "cost" to the employer and thus reduce the attractiveness of labour as opposed to other factors of production such as machinery (the contemporary debate around the potential impact of automation on jobs can be seen in this context). In this schema, a minimum wage, for example, would raise the price of labour and hence reduce labour demand (which is argued to lead to a rise in unemployment). Similar effects would be seen from non-wage labour regulations such as employment protection laws, trade union recognition rights, pension entitlements, mandatory training requirements, sick leave, annual leave, maternity pay and health and safety provisions. It is this logic that has underpinned the many clarion calls (in developed and developing countries alike) for labour market deregulation over the past 30 years.

The countervailing view of employment/labour regulations is that they serve to benefit *both* employers and workers, by introducing minimum standards, encouraging increased productivity and preventing so-called "bad employers" from passing on the social costs of a commodified workforce to the rest of society. A simple example here being that sick leave enables ill workers some time to recover and therefore avoid having to come in to work and potentially passing on their illness to other workers, thereby adversely affecting overall labour productivity.

The extent of labour market regulation and hence government involvement in the employment relationship clearly varies across countries (Lewis *et al.* 2003), ranging from so-called "laissez-faire" arrangements where the only role of government is to uphold property rights and the management–worker relationship is left to individual (i.e., business) prerogative; through to "corporatist", or even "statist" arrangements whereby the government exerts a higher degree, or complete degree of control over every aspect of the employment relationship (*ibid.*).

In extremis, the statist set-up could be equated with an "oligarchical collectivist"[15] society whereby the state owns all the means of production and thus dictates every aspect of the employment relationship. This example today can only be seen in North Korea, whereby laissez-faire economies might be represented by Hong Kong, or the US and UK in milder guises. Hall and Soskice (2001), writing about "varieties of capitalism", denoted a basic distinction between what they termed "liberal market economies" (e.g., the UK, US and south-east Asian economies) and "coordinated market economies" (e.g., Germany, France and Japan). In their schema, liberal market economies were characterized by laissez-faire or voluntary collective bargaining, short-termism and a dominance of "outsider" stakeholder relations in businesses (e.g., shareholders), whilst coordinated market economies were characterized by corporatist or statist arrangements, a longer-term view, and a dominance of "insider" stakeholder relations in business.

This argument notwithstanding, the cut-and-thrust of labour market developments over the past 30 years, having been driven by the intertwining forces of technological change and increased international competition, have been key drivers of labour market and product market deregulation which have combined to erode the significance of the standard employment relationship (SER) in mature industrialized economies (both liberal market economies and coordinated market economies alike) and increase informalization of the formal sector in emerging and developing economies. For developing economies in particular, gig work (at least as depicted in the digital economy) offers opportunities to attract FDI. As Graham *et al.* (2017: 138) note, "jobs can be created for some of the world's poorest by taking advantage of connectivity and the willingness of an increasing number of firms to outsource business processes".

This in turn has had consequences for the regulatory framework that exists in developed economies, which evolved as a key part of the welfare state that emerged from the ashes of the Second World War. The labour regulation framework that evolved in these countries more-or-less emphasized the primacy of the male breadwinner household (although Scandinavian countries were at the vanguard of promoting policies to foster female

---

15. A term used by George Orwell in his novel *Nineteen Eighty-Four* to describe the ultra-totalitarian system of government of the fictional super-state "Oceania", whereby a small elite group jointly (and ruthlessly) controlled every aspect of society.

labour market participation), with strong trade union representation and an emphasis on collective bargaining (often at an industry-wide level) underpinned by Keynesian macroeconomic policies that promoted "full employment" (Standing 1997). In contrast – and to recap – contingent forms of work such as self-employment and casual employment were regarded as part of a residual, declining secondary sector and thus largely lay outside the regulatory framework in industrialized economies.

Indeed, and here we come back to the central premise of this book with regards to the labour market regulatory framework found in developed and developing countries alike: labour market regulations were emblematic of the SER (and the extent of the SER thus determined their scope of coverage), and hence their (near-universal) coverage in developed economies began to shrink with the resurgence in the incidence of contingent forms of work over the last 30 years. Mirroring this decline in the extent of the SER, of course, has been an accompanying decline in trade union densities and also collective bargaining coverage across countries in the past 30 years, as depicted in Tables 4.1 and 4.2 respectively.

Trade union densities have declined across developed countries because of a combination of factors. These have principally consisted of structural changes to industrial composition, which have seen shifts away from traditionally heavily-unionized sectors such as manufacturing, utilities and the public sector, towards services (and attendant feminization of the labour force). However, these have also included regulatory changes in many

Table 4.1 Trade union density by selected countries, 1960–2016 (%)

Country	1960	1991	2011	2016
Australia	50.2	39.7	18.0	14.5
Germany	34.7	36.0	18.5 (2010)	17.0
UK	38.9	38.2	25.8	23.5
Japan	32.3	24.8	19.0	17.3
Italy	24.7	38.7	35.1 (2010)	34.4
Sweden	72.1	79.2	67.7	67.0 (2015)
France	19.6	9.8	7.6 (2008)	7.9 (2015)
United States	30.9	15.5	11.3	10.3
China	–	–	–	44.9 (2015)
India	–	–	12.8 (ILO)	–

Source: 1960–2011: OECD (2012); 2016: ILO (2018).

countries that have curtailed union activities and strength through the abolition of "closed shop" arrangements, restrictions on picketing and secret ballots for industrial action, etc. (e.g., see Machin 1997, for the UK). Or otherwise regulatory changes have made the use of contingent forms of work much easier, which leads to lower union densities because there is much less of an incentive for an individual to join a union when expectations of tenure are limited. As unions were the primary agents to conduct collective bargaining with employers, it should not be surprising that the workplace coverage of collective agreements has generally fallen in tandem (although as collective agreements typically cover all of an eligible workforce in a country – not just union members – collective bargaining coverage should be higher than that of union density; particularly noticeable for France, Italy and Sweden in Table 4.2).

Suffice to say, the trade union movement across countries has been slow to adapt to changes in the composition of employment beginning in the 1980s; with critics suggesting it remained overly focused on permanent full-time (male) workers to the detriment of non-standard (and female) workers until well into the twenty-first century (Ledwith 2012). For feminist scholars in particular, this was indicative of a continued legacy of cultures of "exclusionary masculinity" being predominant in the traditional union movement (*ibid.*). Nonetheless, it is only in the last ten years or so that the

Table 4.2 Collective bargaining coverage, 1990 and 2016 (% share of workforce)

Country	1990	2016
France	92.0	98.5 (2014)
Sweden	89.0	90.0 (2015)
Italy	83.0	80.0 (2015)
Germany	72.0	56.0
Australia	80.0	47.1
UK	54.0	26.3
Japan	23.0	16.7
United States	18.3	11.5
China	–	40.6 (2013)
India	–	–

Source: 1990: OECD Employment Outlook 2012; 2016: ILO 2018 collective bargaining coverage, 1990 and latest year.

union movement has begun to explicitly mobilize to promote the "rights" of non-standard workers (Simms 2010),[16] a point we return to later in the chapter when looking at some recent industrial disputes surrounding gig economy workers.

It is in this context then, that we wish to reiterate that the umbrella of protective employment regulation in mature industrial economies such as the UK that developed over the course of the twentieth century only covered workers primarily designated as "employees" (and permanent full-time ones at that, with the accompanying explicit gender-bias dimension). To recap, the "self-employed" in contrast, have been excluded from this because they have been assumed not to have an employment relationship with clients. However, as seen in Chapter 3, this form of work has experienced something of an increased focus (with the UK being a particularly pronounced example) since the 2008 economic crisis. Accompanied by a growth of other forms of highly contingent work such as temporary agency work and zero-hours contracts, there is thus a clear rationale to explore the regulatory issues surrounding contingent work, which we explore in the next section. In turn, calls for regulation of gig work have gained increasing stridency in recent years (an issue we return to later in the chapter), with, for example, widespread protests from taxi drivers in the UK, France, Malaysia and the United States to the perceived unfair competitive advantages of Uber.

Regulating contingent work

In one sense, the resurgence (or growth) in contingent forms of work, as encapsulated in the current discourse on the gig economy, is illustrative of a form of regulatory catch-up – denoting the prospect that regulatory development spurs corporate innovation in order to evade the statutes of any said particular pieces of regulation. An additional factor to consider with regards to regulating gig work is where the transactions associated with digital platforms cross national boundaries and it could be unclear as to which jurisdiction is applicable for the work done (Graham *et al.* 2017). However,

---

16. For example, the establishment by the UK TUC of a Commission on Vulnerable Employment (CoVE) in 2007, to come up with recommendations to improve the working conditions of precarious workers.

the pressures driving regulatory developments in the various forms of contingent work will vary, and hence it is to these individual forms of work that we now devote attention. Hence, in this chapter we seek to explore regulation and the lived experience of working in the gig economy and consider the issues raised by Aloisi (2016: 656), namely:

> [m]ust workers in the gig-economy continue to be classified as independent contractors? … Are they employees in the light of many criteria that reveal a disguised employment relationship grounded on their disproportionate vulnerability? Or [quoting Prassl & Risak 2016 here] "do they represent a genuinely novel form of work, deserving of its own legal status and regulatory apparatus"?

In the material that follows, we explore regulatory issues pertaining to the four types of work that we examined in Chapter 3. It should be clear that Aloisi's mention of legal status and consequent regulatory apparatus pertains distinctly to the purported "independent" contractor as the archetypal gig economy worker. However, his framing of this debate in terms of overall labour market vulnerability raises issues around a wider raft of regulatory issues concerning contingent workers in general. Hence, it is to these four groupings of workers (casual workers, agency workers, zero-hours contract workers, and dependent contractors) that our attention now turns.

Casual work

Casual work, as noted earlier, is a subset of temporary (fixed-term contract) work that is characterized by the limited duration of the contract, and typically is paid by the number of hours worked. It is thus an extremely contingent form of temporary work, in contrast to regular fixed-term contract work, which has more stable working-time patterns over a given period (i.e., often full-time), and hence is characterized by the limited scope of regulatory coverage across countries. The EU Part-Time Workers Directive, for example, specifically excludes part-time workers employed on a casual basis (ILO 2016: 256) when "objective" reasons for such exclusions exist and the social partners have been "consulted". Such reasons could include not "overburdening" employers which use casuals on very short-term assignments (*ibid.*). As an indicator of the scope of regulation surrounding temporary contract work, the provisions regarding fixed-term contract work are presented in Tables 4.3 and 4.4 for key developed countries and developing countries respectively.

Table 4.3 Provisions regarding fixed-term contract work in key developed countries

Country	Fixed-term contracts prohibited for permanent tasks?	Maximum length of a single fixed-term contract (months)	Maximum length of fixed-term contracts, including renewals (months)
France	Yes	18	18
Germany	No	No limit	No limit
Italy	No	36	36
Spain	Yes	36	48
UK	No	No limit	No limit
Canada	No	No limit	No limit
United States	No	No limit	No limit
Australia	No	No limit	No limit
Japan	No	36	No limit
Russian Federation	Yes	60	60

Source: World Bank 2018.

Note: Japan strictures for Tokyo and Osaka; United States strictures provided for New York and Los Angeles; Russian Federation strictures provided for Moscow and St Petersburg.

In Australia, the lack of employment benefits associated with casual work is meant to be compensated by a top-up to the hourly wage rate. This takes place in the form of an explicit "loading" (that is, penalty rate), generally at 25 per cent of the hourly rate for casual workers (ILO 2016: 64) and ostensibly to compensate for their lack of other key employment entitlements. What is remarkable about this "loading" is that it has survived in a context of some 20 years of market-led labour reforms in Australia. These reforms included the Howard Liberal–National (conservative) government legislating to remove unfair dismissal rights for workers in (corporate) enterprises with less than 100 employees under the auspices of their "Work Choices" industrial relations Act (Chapman 2006). That this legislation was passed prior to the 2007 federal election was widely regarded as a key factor precipitating the downfall of the then government.

Table 4.4 Provisions regarding fixed-term contract work in key developing countries/NICs

Country	Fixed-term contracts prohibited for permanent tasks?	Maximum length of a single fixed-term contract (months)	Maximum length of fixed-term contracts, including renewals (months)
Argentina	Yes	60	60
Brazil	Yes	24	24
Mexico	Yes	No limit	No limit
China	No	No limit	No limit
India	No	No limit	No limit
Indonesia	Yes	24	36
Egypt	No	No limit	No limit
Nigeria	No	No limit	No limit
South Africa	Yes	No limit	No limit
Turkey	Yes	No limit	No limit

Source: World Bank 2018.

Note: Brazil strictures for Rio de Janeiro and Sao Paulo; China strictures for Beijing and Shanghai; India strictures for Delhi and Mumbai; Indonesia strictures for Jakarta and Surabaya; Mexico strictures for Mexico City and Monterrey; Nigeria strictures for Kano and Lagos.

Temporary agency work

In a similar fashion to casual work, temporary agency work is also characterized by a high level of insecurity of tenure. In addition, the ambiguous nature of TWA arrangements meant that it was not always clear who the employer was (Davidov 2004). In the UK, for example, a worker traditionally needed to be both controlled by and have an employment contract with an enterprise in order to be considered as an employee (*ibid.*: 731). If the agency worker did not satisfy both of these criterion, then they might not be covered by certain employment benefits. In an attempt to provide a modicum of basic conditions for agency workers in the EU, the EU issued a Directive to regulate the terms and conditions of temporary agency work. The Temporary Agency Workers' Directive introduced in 2008 was meant to provide some semblance of basic rights for agency workers. However, Ewing (2014: 10) argues that the Directive "was, at best, seeking to reconcile contradictory impulses, to be simultaneously permissive and protective". This was evident in that the Directive also sought to remove restrictions on the use of TAW in countries where it had been previously prohibited, or otherwise tightly regulated (*ibid.*).

Moreover, for Ewing, the drawing up of the Directive was fundamentally compromised in that it did not represent genuine social dialogue at a European level, but rather reflected trade-offs to secure the support of national governments of varying persuasions. This was most notable in the UK, with the then Labour Government only giving assent to the Directive on the premise that a "qualifying period" for equal treatment of agency workers could be inserted, if the social partners agreed to it.[17] It was this trade-off that led to a qualifying period of 12 *continuous* calendar weeks tenure (i.e., in the same *role* with the same *hirer*, and no short breaks in service or rotating staff or job tasks – something that could be easily done by TWAs keen to avoid this stricture) being introduced in the UK before certain entitlements became available to agency workers there. Ewing suggests that the Trades Union Congress (TUC) in the UK only agreed to this qualifying period (removing an estimated 40% of agency workers from coverage) as the price to pay for the UK government agreeing to support the Directive in the first place (*ibid.*: 13).

Thus, interpretation of the EU Directive into national law in member countries has been subject to variation, although all member states have adopted it in a fashion, as depicted in Table 4.5. Indeed, what is notable is that of the countries mentioned in the table, all the current 28 EU member states have at least partially adopted equal treatment of TAW workers. In contrast, countries such as Australia, Canada, Japan, New Zealand, Singapore, South Africa and the United States, do not have this principle enshrined at all in their labour law frameworks (*ibid.*). For a UK contemplating exiting the EU regulatory orbit under the premise of a "hard Brexit", it is indeed notable that such a regulatory divergence occurs between regular and agency work in these largely English-speaking "liberal market" economies. In turn (at the time of writing), this could provide pointers for

---

17. The Blair–Brown Labour Government, in contrast to its predecessor Labour administrations, had embraced labour flexibility as a source of competitive advantage to the UK economy (Brown *et al.*: 2007) and TAWs as a key player in delivering this (McCann 2007) and thus it was wary of inculcating business opposition to any embrace of the TAW Directive.

Table 4.5 Principles of equal treatment for temporary agency work

Type of Limitations	Countries
Basic terms and conditions of employment	Austria*, Belgium, Croatia, Czech Republic, Denmark, Estonia, France, Finland, Germany*, Greece, Iceland, Hungary (6-month qualification period can apply regarding pay), India, Ireland, Israel*, Italy, Latvia, Luxembourg, Mexico, Namibia, Netherlands*, Norway, Peru, Poland, Portugal**, Slovakia, Slovenia, South Korea, Spain, Sweden*, UK (3-month qualifying period applies), Uruguay
Partial	Brazil (pay), China (pay), Colombia, Ethiopia, Romania (pay), Russian Federation (pay), Switzerland
No principle of equal treatment	Australia, Canada, Chile, Japan, New Zealand, Panama, Singapore, South Africa, United States

Source: ILO 2016: 254.

*"Derogations from the principle of equal treatment may be provided for by collective bargaining agreements"

**"After 60 days of work, the collective agreement applied to comparable workers in the user firm applies to agency workers". Questions remain over the EU Directive here in terms of just what constitutes a "comparable worker"; Ewing (2014) suggests some ambiguity here in terms of employer discretion to "define" this. Partial compliance with the principle of equal treatment can be manifest in terms of pay, but not other conditions of work, for example (ibid.).

future labour regulation development in the UK, should abandonment of (or a gradual divergence away from) the EU regulatory framework come to pass.

Ewing (2014) refers to the notion of "effective labour law" – i.e., that such laws should be universal in scope. In this context, we may note that countries that have legislation to promote the equal treatment of agency workers don't always uphold these principles; for example, India, where if non-compliance with this principle has been found to have occurred, then to all purposes, it appears that "there is no obligation of the principle employer to make up any shortfall in payment" (Landau *et al.* 2015; cited in ILO 2016: 254). This and other examples, such as the so-called "Swedish derogation" reported by unions in the UK, whereby agency workers are permanently employed by the TWA in order to avoid equal treatment for pay purposes (*ibid.*: 255) demonstrate that there are various loopholes by which the principles of such regulation can be undermined.

Zero-hours contract work

Zero-hours contract workers are clearly amongst the most vulnerable employees, with recourse to very few employment rights. Ewing (2014: 17) notes that zero-hours contract workers in the UK are unlikely to have protection from unfair dismissal. This is because under UK employment law, to qualify for this, one needs to have two years' continuous tenure in the same job. Whilst legislation can cover for absences due to illness or maternity leave, for example, as not interrupting this two-year qualifying period, it appears that intermittent service/hours worked due to the vagaries of labour demand with a zero-hours contract mean that such workers are unlikely to be afforded such protections (*ibid.*). The concerns around the use, and rapid growth of zero-hours contracts led the UK government in 2015 to make some tentative steps to regulating this form of work by amending the 1996 Employment Rights Act to "render unenforceable any exclusivity clauses preventing zero-hours workers from working for another employer without their employer's consent" (ILO 2016: 260).

However, in contrast to the minimalist regulatory approach taken by the UK, the concerns around the use of zero-hours contracts have been such that some countries have taken particular legislative steps to restrict – or even proscribe – their use completely. The most notable of these was the prohibition of "certain forms" of zero-hours contracts by the New Zealand government in its Employment Relations Act 2016 (ILO 2016: 260), following a concerted campaign by the Unite union and other community groups (Ainge-Roy 2016).

In a more limited fashion, in the United States, eight states and the District of Columbia and Puerto Rico have introduced "reporting time pay" laws that require firms to pay employees for a guaranteed minimum number of hours, typically three or four, "when they report for a scheduled shift" (ILO 2016: 259) regardless of whether the actual time worked is less. This applies even if the said employee turns up for a shift that is subsequently cancelled or reduced (*ibid.*). Similarly, in the Netherlands, those working under 15 hours per week could receive some entitlements if they have work schedules which are "not fixed" or if the "number of working hours is not clearly determined", then workers should at least receive three hours' paid work, regardless of how many hours they actually reported (*ibid.*). Similarly, in Germany, "on-call" contracts must specify the minimum hours of work on a daily or weekly basis, and if this is not explicitly stipulated, then authorities will assume that an implied working week of ten hours will have been agreed, and a minimum of three hours should be paid per shift, regardless of the actual number of hours worked (*ibid.*).

Dependent contractors

Many of the concerns with zero-hours contract work can also be reiterated for dependent contractors. Indeed, dependent contractors, as we have noted throughout this book, are amongst the most vulnerable workers when it comes to derogation of employment rights, as they are not generally recognized as employees across countries. However, whilst the legislative framework surrounding dependent contractors and any employment rights across countries appears to be largely lacking, there are actually instances where such workers could have recourse to *some* employment rights. In the UK, for example, Section 230(3) of the 1996 Employment Rights Act defined two categories (or "limbs") of workers for this purpose (see the judgment of the Supreme Court of the UK, 2014):

Limb (a) comprised of persons who essentially had entered into a contract of employment (as depicted in a clearly defined hierarchical relationship with an organisation);

Limb (b) consisted of those persons who "worked under any other contract, whether express or implied and (if it is express) whether oral or in writing, whereby the individual undertakes to do or perform *personally* any work or services for another party to the contract whose status is not by virtue of the contract that of a client or customer of any profession or business undertaking carried on by the individual" (Judgment of Lady Hale, *ibid.*: 2, emphasis added).

As such, Limb (b) workers were also entitled to the right "not to suffer unauthorized deduction from wages (Section 13)" and also "the right not be subject to a detriment for exercising rights under the Working Time Regulations" (Section 45A)[18] (*ibid.*: 3). This does seem to suggest that such gig workers should be able to (in theory) have some control over the frequency and patterns of their work assignments. Moreover, the emphasis on *personally* undertaking a service denoted above clearly puts them in a distinct position to other contractors, who (in theory again) could hire other people to undertake work on their behalf. These workers then, under UK law, were also entitled to a modicum of other benefits, namely, annual leave, a minimum wage, and anti-discrimination laws (Moyer-Lee 2018).

As such, Aloisi (2016: 663) observes that workers denoted as independent contractors in the gig economy have been increasingly turning to suing their platform providers (e.g., Uber, or cleaning firm Handy) for "inappropriately classifying them as contractors although they do not enjoy the amount of freedom that the label is supposed to entail" (*ibid.*). That this is occurring should not be surprising (as Aloisi notes), as unions in particular have become increasingly vocal in articulating what they regard as the highly precarious nature of these work arrangements in that all risk is transferred onto the worker for what they regard as a proxy regular employment relationship. And as inferred from the provisions of the UK 1996 Employment Rights Act, the judiciary have acted to uphold these laws where they exist.

What then emerges in the court cases arising from the interpretation of these judgments is that platform providers could seek to evade the provisions of the 1996 Act by inserting a supplementary clause "allowing" the gig worker to have someone else work on their behalf and thereby evade coverage of the Act. However, Moyer-Lee (2018) argues that "tribunals and courts usually see through this nonsense". In other words, that the key feature in attributing these employment rights is that the "dominant feature of the contract" is one that makes clear that the gig worker must be the person essentially doing the work (*ibid.*). The issues surrounding creeping regulation of gig workers across a number of countries are depicted in Box 4.1 below.

The misrepresentation of workers as independent contractors has prompted some countries (even those with common law legal systems) to

---

18. At the time of writing, the regulations from the Working Time Directive are particularly contentious in the UK, with the looming advent of Brexit and the likelihood that any post-Brexit UK government will seek to reduce the scope of employment rights arising from this directive (Salh *et al.* 2017).

BOX 4.1 REGULATION IS HAPPENING

- Gig workers in October 2018 staged a number of strikes across the UK in protest over pay. Companies affected included Wetherspoons, McDonalds, Uber Eats and TGI Fridays. The strikes were coordinated across a number of regions including South America, the Philippines, Japan and parts of Europe (BBC News, 4 October 2018). As a result, there have been signs that gig companies are being subjected to increasing critical scrutiny.
- In the UK the Taylor Review of Modern Working Practices (July 2017) concluded that all work should be fair and prompted the UK government to assert that workers rights will be "strictly enforced" (BBC News, 11 July 2017).
- In the UK Uber lost a court appeal and received the judgment that drivers should be treated as employees (BBC News, 10 November 2011); the same judgment occurred in California where drivers were deemed to be employees and not contractors (BBC News, 17 June 2015).
- The Court of Justice of the European Union stated in 2017 that Uber is a taxi firm and therefore subject to all the same regulations as any other company (BBC News, 20 December 2017).
- In December 2017, Uber's licence was suspended in Sheffield following the company's failure to provide data after official requests (BBC News, 7 December 2017). The supension was subsequently lifted.
- In September 2017 Uber lost its licence to operate in London with one MP stating that Uber was "morally wrong" (BBC News, 11 July 2017). In June 2018 Uber won its appeal to overturn the ban.

The willingness of authorities to engage critically with gig companies is for some a positive sign, but for others it is a diminution of choice both for consumers and workers.

---

impose by statute, certain measures to try and prevent this. For example, the then Australian Labor (Federal) Government, in its Fair Work Act 2009, which proscribed:

> misrepresenting an employment relationship as an independent contracting arrangement; dismissing or threatening to dismiss an employee for the purposes of re-engaging them as an independent contractor; or making a knowingly false statement to persuade or

influence an employee to become an independent contractor" (ILO 2016: 262).

However, none of these developments should detract from the essentially highly precarious nature of such work arrangements. In terms of Standing's (1997) typology of labour security – and the adaptation by De Ruyter and Burgess (2003) to explore labour insecurity – dependent contractors have virtually no security on any of these indicators; be it labour market, employment, work, job, income, skill reproduction, or union representation. It is thus to the "lived experience" of such forms of work that we now turn.

The "lived experience" of working in the gig economy

The regulatory issues highlighted in previous sections have underlined the essentially vulnerable position of workers in the gig economy. The controversies surrounding the use – and rapid growth of – these forms of work in the UK were such that a government-commissioned review into "modern working practices" resulted in recommendations that the government: 1) entitle workers to "a written statement of employment particulars"; 2) lower the "Information and Consultation of Employees (ICE) threshold"[19]; and 3) end the "Swedish Derogation" for agency workers (UK Parliament 2018).[20] Even where such workers enter into gig working arrangements of their own choice, the balance of bargaining power lies with the platform provider, or "employer".

---

19. The ICE provisions relate to the EU Directive on Information and Consultation of Employees, which seeks to impart "minimum principles, definitions and arrangements for information and consultation of employees at the enterprise level within each country" for those enterprises with a minimum of 50 employees (or a minimum of 20 employees if an individual member country desired it). Such (enterprise-wide) items for consultation could include information on the financial viability of the enterprise, potential for redundancies, or other aspects of major organizational change. See http://ec.europa.eu/social/main.jsp?catId=707&langId=en&intPageId=210 (accessed 31 July 2018).
20. See the The Taylor Review of Modern Working Practices at: https://publications.parliament.uk/pa/cm201719/cmselect/cmworpen/352/35204.htm#_idText Anchor005 (accessed 29 July 2018).

This only serves to reiterate the precarious nature of such work. In this context, one striking finding from the ILO (2016: 188) was that in respect to non-standard employment being a "bridge" to standard employment; in the "vast majority" of countries examined, this was only the case for less than 55 per cent of such workers – and in some cases, less than 10 per cent (*ibid.*). For graduates, migrant workers and those "initially disadvantaged" with low education or earnings, these effects were particularly pronounced (*ibid.*). What this suggests is that the gig economy, rather than being the manifestation of some choice-theoretic freelancer ideal, is more typified by workers caught in cycles of precarious employment, alternating with spells of unemployment. Indeed, such workers were more likely to transition into unemployment or economic inactivity than those in permanent full-time work (*ibid.*: 189).

Hence, in this section, we wish to complete our examination of the gig economy by examining some aspects of the actual working conditions attached to gig work. In doing this, we use the template provided by Graham *et al.* (2017), with reference to their "four concerns for digital labour", namely: bargaining power, economic exclusion, intermediation, and finally, implications for skill and capability development (*ibid.*).

Bargaining power

The income associated with gig work is generally regarded as low compared to (employed) wage labour, and hence all the forms of work surveyed in this chapter are generally characterized by a high degree of income inse-curity (Standing 1997). In this context, we may note the analysis of the Resolution Foundation on self-employed workers in the UK in 2016, which suggested that approximately 50 per cent of these were low paid and took home less than two-thirds of median earnings. Furthermore, two million self-employed workers in the UK were reported as earning less than £8.00 per hour (not far off the current national minimum wage/national living wage of £7.83 per hour for an adult over the age of 25).[21]

However, in developing countries this is not necessarily the case. Graham *et al.* (2017) argue that for workers in these countries, income associated with

---

21. See https://www.gov.uk/national-minimum-wage-rates (accessed 27 July 2018).

digital platform work can exceed that of full-time jobs in their own countries – one example they cite from their research was that of a Filipino respondent who was a mathematics lecturer in Manila who quit his full-time job in 2011 to undertake search engine optimization for US clients at an hourly rate of $4.00 (*ibid.*: 144). The individual concerned reported earning almost three times his previous salary and enjoyed his work (*ibid.*), suggesting that such forms of work can, sometimes at least, be beneficial. However, this was not necessarily typical. Graham *et al.* (2017: 145) also noted the "fierce" competition between digital platform workers to secure work, which often resulted in workers underbidding one another; and a sense of general powerlessness in contemplating asking for a pay rise with "employers" able to impose arbitrary changes in contract. As such, they noted that "many employers can easily practice 'labour arbitrage', that is, buy labour from where it is cheapest. This can reduce the market power of workers relative to employers and put downward pressure on labour prices" (*ibid.*).

Economic exclusion

Graham *et al.* (2017: 146) define "economic exclusion" in terms of labour market discrimination due to some personal characteristic such as religion or ethnicity, or otherwise in terms of occupational segregation due to characteristics such as gender. For Graham *et al.* (*ibid.*), the use of a digital platform to mediate work potentially allowed for such workers to "access their local market through a veil of anonymity provided by the digital medium, masking the characteristic on which discrimination occurs" (*ibid.*: 147).

In contrast, Lee (2017) suggests that workers in highly contingent work arrangements typified in the gig economy (particularly those on zero-hours contracts, for whom this work is likely to be the main source of income) might not have sufficient stability of earnings over a given period to secure certain forms of financial payments (e.g., direct debits). This is not insignificant; citing a Save the Children study (2011), Lee suggests that if "low-income families could afford direct debits [rather than, e.g., having to use pre-payment meters], safe in the knowledge they could afford the monthly costs, they would save on average £250 a year" (*ibid.*: 30). This is particularly relevant to disadvantaged groups such as women, who are more likely to be over-represented in such forms of work and want a permanent and/or full-time job (ILO 2016: 186).

Intermediation

Graham *et al.* (2017) note that "value capture" is a significant activity for those involved in production in global value chains, and that intermediaries play an important role in this process by dint of "geographic location, networks, and other positional advantages to mediate between buyers and sellers" (*ibid.*: 149). For Graham *et al.*, (*ibid.*) digital platforms could potentially allow workers to "circumvent" some of these intermediaries and thereby improve their relative labour market position. However, the authors also found that digital platforms could lead to "re-intermediation", whereby some platform workers would be able to take on, or subcontract, to other platform workers. In some cases, such individuals were reported by respondents to be "more exploitative" than end-clients, often demanding completed work in a matter of hours, rather than days, and "paid workers only a small fraction of what they themselves received for the tasks" (*ibid.*: 150).

Implications for skill and capability development

For Graham *et al.* (2017: 151), alleviating the effects of intermediation (i.e., "disintermediation") could increase the scope for digital platform workers to "attempt to perform higher value-added services" (*ibid.*). However (citing Pietrobelli & Rabellotti 2011), they note that IT outsourcing could also act as an inhibitor to platform (gig) workers via them being denied contextual knowledge about tasks outsourced through these platforms (*ibid.*). They found that such digital platform workers were often undertaking tasks that did not match their skill sets; i.e., that such workers in effect were over-qualified for the work that they were being asked to do (*ibid.*: 152). Findings such as this raise wider concerns over the returns to (higher) education that now accrue to such workers across the world.

Indeed, it is evident that such forms of work are typified by all the risks being displaced onto the gig economy worker, including the costs of any training. Indeed, given the contingent nature of gig work, there is no incentive for a platform provider/employer to invest in a worker whose link to the firm is transient at best. For Friedman (2014) this poses a fundamental conundrum for capitalist economies, as traditionally, internal labour markets:

> bridged the gap between private interest and public. [However] the rise of the gig economy blows this bridge … If companies do not invest in worker training, they may have to rely more on worker threats and punishments, higher rates of unemployment, and cost-of-job loss to maintain continued work effort … such punitive measures cannot elicit creative and innovative work. (*ibid.*: 183).

This finding suggests then, that the overall ramifications for growth of the gig economy – and its effects on other parts of economies around the world – in all likelihood will be negative for productivity and skills acquisition.

Summary

In this chapter, we have looked behind headline figures to examine the actual nature of the regulatory framework that shapes work in the gig economy, and also therefore to examine the lived experience faced by gig workers. In particular in this chapter, we have sought to get under the label of "independent contractor" often used by gig economy firms to describe their workforce, in order to show that often such individuals are dependent contractors, and thus entitled to a basic level of employment rights.

In *extremis*, the commodified, contingent nature of the work has served to erode the traditional boundaries between work time and personal time, to the extent that platform providers such as WeWork (who offer office space on a pro-rata basis for transient profician gig workers) are moving into the business of providing co-located living and work spaces, under a spin-off enterprise titled WeLive (Harris 2018). WeWork present a number of benefits to accompany the hire of office space, which Harris reports as "free beer on tap, regular pilates sessions, and more" (*ibid.*). The image here then appears to be one of purporting to sell an attractive communal lifestyle to footloose freelancers who otherwise would feel dislocated from any sense of community and belonging that comes with a stable job in one area. In-kind benefits such as this, or those provided by Google to its workers, such as free meals and recreational spaces, must be caveated with the notion that such benefits are obviously used to elicit greater commitment and effort from workers. In this context, it is notable that some workers were reported in 2012 as living on-site at Google HQ (in Santa Clara County, California) in a caravan (even if rent-free), and working up to 90 hours per week (Collman 2014).

As the examples above attest, the growth of the gig economy and its potential for eroding the employment terms and conditions of work in other sectors, then, poses a direct challenge to the agendas of international organizations such as the ILO, who seek to promote the growth of "decent work" (ILO 2016). In this context, the ILO define "decent work" as:

> work that is productive and delivers a fair income, with a safe workplace and social protection, better prospects for social development and integration, freedom for people to express their concerns, organize and participate in the decisions that affect their lives and equality of opportunity and fair treatment for all women and men. (2016: 247).

The Decent Work Agenda, as formalized in the ILO's 2008 Declaration on Social Justice for a Fair Globalization (see Ewing, 2014, for a discussion) has four key aspects; job creation; developing sustainable measures of social protection (including labour protection and *enforcement* thereof); promotion of social dialogue and tripartism in national systems of labour relations (e.g., as with the EU's social partners industrial relations approach); and "respect, promotion and realisation of the fundamental principles and rights at work" (*ibid.*: 3–4). As inferred earlier, it is highly problematic to see how such principles could be applied to a group of workers who have been consistently referred by their user companies as non-employees, in order to avoid being subject to labour regulation. In this sense, for Ewing (2014: 20), "commodification is a direct result of labour law's *ineffectiveness*, a consequence of the failure to *ensure* the robust application of the first principle that labour law should be universal in its scope" (*ibid.*, emphasis added). Indeed (as this chapter has evidenced), it could be said that the basic structural premises of gig work are antithetical to the very premise of "decent work" (that is, de-commodified), as defined by the ILO.

This leads us to consider, in the final chapter of this book, the highly commodified nature of work carried out in the gig economy, and what the implications will be for individuals, organizations and the wider society going forward, as the technology underpinning gig work continues to evolve. Above all is a need to urgently reconsider our relationship towards

---

BOX 4.2 THE CHANGING STRATEGY OF GIG COMPANIES

- Uber's strategy has included, for example, the use of Greyball software to identify and deny services to certain riders, including local government regulators trying to "catch them out" (BBC News, 4 March 2017).
- Uber has also faced Google in court over allegedly stealing critical intellectual property related to Google's driverless car technology, Waymo (BBC News, 16 May 2018).
- Deliveroo reportedly encourages its employees to avoid using language that might imply that a permanent contractual relationship exists, for example, workers are termed "independent suppliers" and uniforms are "kit" or "equipment" and workers who do not attend a shift are deemed to have been "unavailable" (BBC News, 5 April 2017).

However, in response to pressure and legal attention the gig companies appear to be softening their approach.

- Uber, for example, accepted the need for change following the loss of their licence in London and stopped using the Greyball software (BBC News, 9 March 2018).
- They have also stated that they want to "make its employees happier" and offered sick pay and parental leave (BBC News, 21 March 2017).
- In the US the company have added a tipping option to their Uber App (BBC News, 17 April 2017).
- On an international level Uber sold its food delivery services in Singapore and China to local competitors (BBC News, 26 March 2018).
- In April 2017, Uber pulled out of Denmark altogether after new taxi laws were introduced (BBC News, 28 March 2017).
- There were even signs of disunity within Uber when company president, Jeff Jones stood down in March 2017 following disagreements over styles of leadership with the then CEO Travis Kalanick (BBC News, 20 March 2017).

Whether this change of approach is the result of pressure from the workers, or government (or both) is difficult to say, but perhaps there is much more to come.

"the market" and to what extent untrammelled market forces should dictate economic and social well-being in an increasingly polarized, segmented workforce. As Ewing (2014: 9) argues, "[s]egmentation reinforces commodification, and indeed helps to create extreme forms of commodification". For countries such as the UK, struggling to emerge from the 2008 financial crisis, and subsequent "austerity" macroeconomic policies, now followed by the political turmoil brought about by "Brexit", these issues are all the more acute (Lee 2017). In this sense, we may note that the changes wrought by technology, globalization and deregulation – as encapsulated in the gig economy – and the subsequent populist backlash of Brexit, "Trumpism" (Piketty 2016) and a general resurgence of the far right in politics across the globe, are not unrelated.

This is not to suggest that gig companies will forever effectively lie outside the purview of regulation. As the examples earlier of gig worker industrial action attest, the re-commodification of labour in the gig economy has generated opposition, and platform providers such as Uber, have had to adjust their business model across countries (see Box 4.2). However, it is likely that the sector will continue to develop labour-saving technologies. As such, it raises the rather disturbing question of what other forms of "disruption" lie in wait just around the corner for societies caught between the challenges wrought by automation, inequality and the prospect of severe environmental degradation brought about by climate change. Can capitalism survive these challenges? In the last chapter, we consider some of these issues.

5

Conclusions and implications: from wage economy to gig economy to automated ("no") economy?

This book has sought to get behind the contemporary buzz and rhetoric around the use of the terms "gig", "gig work" and "gig economy". In so doing, we have attempted to provide some theoretical and empirical analysis of the gig work phenomenon, to assess critically some of the rhetorical claims made about gig work, and to develop a more objective stance on gig work by looking at more robust academic work exploring this, and related areas.

In Chapter 1 we examined origins of the term "gig" and contemporary definitions of the gig economy by looking closely at one of the most common environments in which we see the word used: the music business. We noted that key features of the music business were also very apparent in the gig economy. Chapter 2 anchored the concept of the gig economy to theoretical work on segmented labour markets and labour flexibility to illustrate that in many respects there is nothing new about the gig economy – that it could be seen as "old wine in a new bottle". Chapter 3 operationalized the concept of gig work in various forms of contingent work – casual work, agency work, zero-hours contracts and dependent contractors – to shine a light on trends we appear to be seeing in the UK and other parts of the world: a (post-2008 economic crisis) resurgence in short-term and precarious work. Our analysis revealed that not only is gig work not new, but also that its growth was in some sense predictable. Chapter 4 then examined the regulatory framework as pertains to gig workers, and also aspects of their "lived experience". Evident here was that labour law frameworks had struggled to keep abreast with developments in the gig economy, as their coverage was historically rooted to the premise that a worker has to be an employee to be covered by employment rights.

This final chapter offers a critique of the idea that the market is acting as a benevolent allocator of resources. The fundamental apologia typically offered in defence of the gig economy is that it is the result of the workings of the market and since the market is so often regarded as the *summum bonum* of human social achievement, the gig economy is a "win-win" development in labour relations. However, aided and abetted by technology, the gig economy proceeds with winners and losers in its wake.

The gig economy and societal values

The gig economy appears to be symptomatic of a structural shift in the workings of advanced post-industrial societies. We have seen that trade unions are weaker than at any time in the past 50 years and that work itself is increasingly fragmented and precarious. Gig economy work is characterized by short-term or even zero-hours contracts, which has allowed companies to call on people to carry out work at a moment's notice. In the past this was more common in some occupations than others, for example, the pub trade has long employed people with very little notice of their shifts, and as we have seen, the existence of such working arrangements and employer–employee relations has been with us for centuries (Harvey *et al.* 2017).

In contrast to the earlier debates around the "primary" and "secondary sectors" highlighted in the discussion on the dual labour market (Doeringer & Piore 1971) in Chapter 2, what appears to be new is the extension of this into more and more areas of work and indeed far beyond relatively low-skilled work into the "professions". For example, university lecturers are now frequently hired on a sessional basis depending on the demand for their particular skills from students in a particular academic year. This demand fluctuates and so, therefore, does the demand for specialist lecturers in different fields. This is institutionalized in UK schools where the notion of the "supply teacher" is well established, but while the sessional university lecturer has also been with us for a long time, in the past it was seen as a way to cover short-term skills problems, now it appears to be a structural part of university recruitment activity. This shift has been accompanied and facilitated by a number of other developments, for example, publishers increasingly require authors of text books to produce books with accompanying "ancillaries" – visuals, case-studies and teaching and learning aids – that enable any reasonably competent lecturer to deliver lectures to large numbers of students without having specialist knowledge in the field. The same movement towards atomization and deskilling can be seen in a number of professions and prompts the questions: are we seeing a broader and more pervasive shift in the world of work? And, if so, what might be causing it?

The idea that the gig economy is a manifestation of a change in work and employment relations could also reflect a movement in deeper societal values. This is supported by the observations of the American sociologist, George Ritzer (1993), who argued that our society has become dominated by organizations whose driving ambition is to achieve four main objectives: efficiency, calculability, predictability and control. Ritzer acknowledges his intellectual debt to the German sociologist, Max Weber, who at the start of the twentieth century identified the growth of bureaucratization in our organizations and its dehumanizing effects. Ritzer's contention is that the chief objective of organizations is the achievement of efficiency, to this, all other aims are subordinated. Ritzer's seminal work, *The McDonaldization of Society* explores this drive in the twentieth century and concludes that the rationality of this is eventually undermined, as the "irrationality of the rational" becomes apparent. For example, pushing workers to the limit physically and emotionally in an attempt to be more efficient, eventually results in more sickness and absenteeism leading to high staff turnover and higher costs in recruitment and training. Still, it is seen as good for business in the short term. The push for efficiency, for example, means a preoccupation with counting the difference between the inputs and the outputs.

Is the gig economy "win-win"?

The shift in values we may be witnessing is perhaps given a boost of credibility by the presentation of the gig economy as a "win-win" situation. Indeed, gig work is usually presented as self-evidently a good thing, perhaps even, the future of work. The various stakeholders are getting what they want from it: gig workers are getting flexible working arrangements that enable them to work in a variety of situations to suit their needs. They are paid according to the work they do, which is an incentive to work harder and longer. This benefits the employer, who gets workers when they need them and by increasing competition among workers drives down labour costs, reducing overheads and offers loopholes that enable them to circumvent some of the costs of a permanent labour force (such as pensions, paid leave and redundancy payments).

The benefits of the gig economy, it is argued, proceed from the workings of a free market. The workers are free to choose what work they do, when and for whom. Employers can hire as and when they need to, flexing to consumer demand. The consumers are equally free to choose what they buy or what service they use, how much and from whom. In the absence of any external influence on the price, according to orthodox economic theory of the market, supply and demand will eventually equate. Seen in this way, the largely unregulated activity of companies operating in the gig economy is beneficial to all members of society. In turn the gig economy has added further novelty to the workings of the market by its ability to take consumption goods such as cars and turn them into monetized goods in the provision of a service (Kenney & Zysman 2016).

As such, the market has been held up to be the single best allocator of resources since the eighteenth century. Since Adam Smith's *Wealth of Nations* published in 1776, most have come to believe that the market is the best way to ensure that people have what they need and/or want. And, paradoxically, that came not from concern for others but from self-interest: "It is not from the benevolence of the butcher, the brewer, or the baker that we expect our dinner, but from their regard to their own interest" (Smith 1776/1982).

From the observation that our self-interest will lead to an improvement in the economic well-being of others springs a number of policy prescriptions. For example, the idea that if we leave the economy alone (laissez-faire) its workings, via self-interested people, will benefit everyone. Conversely, if we interfere with it we will be worse off collectively. Thus, free market proponents argue that any government interference in the activities of business, and therefore the market, would most likely lead to a diminution of the economic prosperity of individuals, whether in business or not. Milton Friedman (1979) argued we are "Free to Choose" and what we choose will be supplied if we are able and willing to pay for it. There is a simple elegance to this idea: in a perfect market where people are free to choose, the right amount will be supplied at a price people are able and willing to pay. There is also an element of democracy buried in here too. Money becomes a voting currency. On this basis, the gig economy is supplying goods and services which are in demand (where demand is the willingness and ability to pay) and in addition, people doing gig work are also free to choose whether to work under these conditions or not.

However, in the real world, for many people this simply might not be a choice. They have to work because they have dependents, financial commitments, or circumstances that mean they cannot turn down the offer of employment, regardless of the terms and conditions. The rise in gig workers has masked true levels of under-employment and enables politicians in the UK, for example, to claim that more people are in work than ever before. But the rise of in-work poverty that is becoming prevalent among those classed as "just-about managing" belies this claim (Coates 2018). Precarious work and low-quality, badly paid jobs that have gradually been replacing long-term, permanent, regulated jobs in our post-industrial economy are having knock-on effects for our society (not least in the rise of dependence on food banks by sections of society).

Here lies the central conflict: in an abstract world the free market would solve all our allocative problems, in a real world, it does not. So, should gig work be regulated or not? Should we regulate to control its development, which some see as a "conspiracy against the public", exploiting working people and their vulnerability, or should we let the market decide on the basis that it is the best means by which we can allocate resources to what the people want?

Whilst "free marketeers" claim that if left alone the market will deliver a social optimum, others argue that in the absence of intervention markets will deliver less than optimum social benefits. Fleming (2017), for example, argues that the human capital literature has largely led to the "radical responsibilitization" of the workforce where workers are seen as individual capitalists responsible for their own socio-economic well-being. However, he argues this can also lead to economic insecurity, low productivity, diminishing autonomy, and rising personal debt. The idea that workers are the authors of their own fortunes ignores the way power works in society and in organizations. Workers are disempowered by such "flexible" arrangements. Begging the question who these arrangements are flexible for? In Fleming's own words: "One cannot truly express individuality, self-reliance and choice when desperately dependent on an unequal power relationship. Wider societal backup and support is necessary" (2017: 703).

Where the power lies, is the central point for many. Michael Porter (1985), for example, argues that the strategic goal of all organizations should be to gain as much power in the market place as possible in an endeavour to "capture" the value being created, regardless of whether or not your own company created it. It is the main pursuit for Porter and the main problem for Fleming. In Fleming's words:

> human capital theory is just one manifestation of a set of comprehensive neoclassical economic ideas that accentuate self-interested individualism as the only way to envisage the organization of work. However, when set upon the backdrop of wider socio-economic inequalities and uneven power relationships, this excessive individualism recasts workers as complete owners of their economic failure. Governments too have followed this policy in relation to training and education. As a result, it is misleading to say that human capital theory is about investing in people. It may also represent a form of divestment. The advocates of Uberization claim it is the future, no matter what. How employees, organizations and scholars respond to this proclamation will shape the politics of work to come (2017: 705).

The experience of the gig worker is worth considering. In a survey of gig work across three online piecework platforms, Lehdonvirta (2018) found that while the work apparently affords the worker considerable flexibility in how they use their time, in reality there are considerable structural constraints around this, which relate to the availability of work and the degree to which workers are dependent upon it. Although it may appear that there is time to do other things, that time to do other things is largely determined by the company, begging the question, "flexible for who"? Similarly, if work is not always available then workers are compelled to take it when they can and not when they want to. In addition to job instability, wages can be insufficient to meet the cost of living forcing gig workers to attempt to juggle more than one job (Drahokoupil *et al.* 2017).

The longer term disbenefits are more apparent in the very vocal opposition to Uber from non-Uber drivers in various countries, not just in the UK. Across many countries, we have seen examples of taxicab drivers who have protested publically against what they regard as erosion of their incomes by firms such as Uber, who they argue do not comply with terms and conditions attached to the sector (BBC 2018; *Evening Standard* 2018; Reuters 2018). This in turn has created a modicum of collective identity amongst taxi drivers and propelled calls for minimum terms and conditions to be attached to all drivers, irrespective of whether they work in a traditional cab, or via a gig platform. Conversely, Uber drivers have protested against what they regard as Uber unilaterally reducing terms in response to new car-share entrants in the market (*Guardian Australia* 2018).

All this underscores that the market does not work perfectly, it will always be the most human of institutions and as such, will always concentrate power in the hands of the few at the expense of the many, if left unregulated. While the UK at least has robust employment laws, gig work, some would argue, nevertheless takes advantage of weaknesses that allow corporations to reap the benefits of "employing" people on a casual basis to avoid the usual associated costs for pensions, paid holiday, redundancy and maternity leave among other entitlements.

The future of the gig economy

Whilst the argument that the gig economy is the result of "market forces" has some credence, we have suggested in this book that its rise as a *structural* element of society could be the result of its alignment with underpinning contemporary societal values (values intimately defined by the notions of convenience and recourse to novel technologies in day-to-day life). But what about the future? Will a fragmented and atomised workforce doing multiple jobs and yet still dependant on large corporations for work be the "way of the future"? Will they still be valued in the years to come? In seeking to at least adequately address these questions, it is necessary to take a step back and consider in some more detail the exact nature of the new technologies that are doing so much to drive developments in the gig economy and wider society.

We have noted that automation and digitalization are having a transformative effect on production and work organization across mature and emerging economies alike. These changes have been argued to constitute a "Fourth Industrial Revolution" (4IR) – a revolution that has been epitomized by such technologies being "seamlessly embedded into our physical environment" (Philbeck & Davis 2019: 18). The 4IR then builds on the "Third Industrial Revolution", which saw the development of digital technologies, and this in turn built on the "Second Industrial Revolution" of electrical power and telecommunications (*ibid.*). However, the 4IR promises far more dramatic changes to society, or even what it means to be human, than just the widespread application of machine-learning algorithms. For Philbeck and Davis, the digital technologies associated with 4IR, when "combined with advanced imaging, signal processing and gene-editing … have the *potential to influence our physiological condition and faculties*" (*ibid.*, our emphasis).

As such, these technological developments have the potential to render many of today's jobs redundant. New technological developments in areas such as robotic process automation (RPA), drones, the internet of things (IoT), artificial intelligence (AI) and machine learning are continuing to impact upon production and society. A complete account of these technologies is beyond the scope of this book, but Box 5.1 provides brief definitions of some of these. What is evident with these technologies is their *intimate complementarity* and that use of one invariably invokes use of another. Drones, for example, could easily be used by an online retailer such as Amazon in concert with the IoT and/or an RPA to entirely remove the human worker element from purchasing and despatching a product to a customer.

Suffice to say, some writers predict that in 10–20 years, half of all current jobs will be "threatened by algorithms" and that "40% of today's top 500 companies will have vanished in a decade" (Helbing *et al.* 2017: 3). Similarly,

---

BOX 5.1 BASIC TECHNOLOGIES ASSOCIATED WITH THE 4IR

- Artificial intelligence (AI):

"An area of computer science that emphasizes the creation of intelligent machines that work and react like humans. Some of the activities computers with artificial intelligence are designed for include: Speech recognition; Learning; Planning; and; Problem solving" (Technopedia 2019). AI can in turn be denoted as "weak AI" (current technology), whereby computers can only simulate the human cognitive function, but are not "conscious" (Technopedia 2019b), and "strong AI", which posits that it could be possible to construct computers that mimic all aspects of the human mind (Technopedia 2019c; still hypothetical at the time of writing).

- The internet of things (IoT):

"A collection of digital technologies, including sensors, communication modules, and various software applications, that all together can digitally integrate analog physical systems with the digital world, providing constant and readily available information about those systems" (Chou 2019: 107–08). An example here would be the platform technology deployed by Uber to connect drivers and users in real time (*ibid*.).

- Machine learning:

"An artificial intelligence (AI) discipline geared toward the technological development of human knowledge. Machine learning allows computers to handle new situations via analysis, self-training, observation and experience. Machine learning facilitates the continuous advancement of computing through exposure to new scenarios, testing and adaptation, while employing pattern and trend detection for improved decisions in subsequent (though not identical) situations" (Technopedia 2019d).

- Robotic process automation (RPA):

"RPA allows the creation of scripted 'robots' that will automate existing [human] processes. The robot acts as a human agent and can interact with other software in the same way a human does. An RPA robot does not make complex decisions without some detailed configuration, but it can quickly and effectively copy repetitive actions allowing for faster and more accurate completion of tasks" (Taylor 2018: 11). An example of an RPA is the automation of routine financial services processes (*ibid*.).

- Drones:

"A drone, in technological terms, is an unmanned aircraft. Drones are more formally known as unmanned aerial vehicles (UAVs) or unmanned aircraft systems (UASes). Essentially, a drone is a flying robot that can be remotely controlled or fly autonomously through software-controlled flight plans in their embedded systems, working in conjunction with onboard sensors and GPS" (Rouse 2019).

Frey and Osborne (2013), basing their article on John Maynard Keynes' (1933) famous prediction of "widespread technological unemployment" (*ibid.*: 2), and citing MGI 2013, suggested that algorithms "could substitute for approximately 140 million full-time knowledge workers world-wide" (*ibid.*: 19). Bonin *et al.* (2015; cited in Schroeder 2016: 4), applying the Frey and Osborne methodology to Germany, suggested that 42 per cent of jobs there could be at risk of automation over a 20-year period. Schroeder suggests that if one considers "activities" instead of "professions" then the predictions are less dramatic – with only 12 per cent of jobs in Germany being at risk. Nevertheless, the expectant job losses would still fall disproportionately on the low-skilled and low-paid (*ibid.*).

Gig economy companies such as Uber have been at the vanguard of developments here; for example, testing prototypes of driverless taxicabs (Goodall *et al.* 2017). While this technology is still in its infancy, it is developing, and Deloitte estimate that by 2040, "up to 80% of passenger miles travelled in urban areas could be in shared autonomous vehicles" (*ibid.*: 122). Similarly, with the use of drone technology, companies such as Amazon and DHL have been piloting the use of these unmanned aerial vehicles to deliver packages, for example (Gharibi *et al.* 2016). Of course, as the number of drones rises over the thousands, the attendant implications for airspace management could yet limit their widespread use, particularly in (crowded) urban areas. However, the labour-saving potential of such devices is still evident in the elimination of any need for someone to transport the goods in question.

Of course, such predictions should be treated with a modicum of caution, as technology can create new jobs as well as destroy current ones (Nübler 2016), so estimating the size of any job-displacement is problematic. Wondering where new jobs would come from, however, to replace jobs lost to automation is equally problematic, as we cannot fathom that everyone will be – or want to be – a "symbolic analyst" (Reich 1991),[22] or a creative

---

22. "Symbolic analysts" were defined by Reich as those who work in the production of "ideas and meaning" (Levi-Faur 1997). Such individuals operate in the networked economy to "design new global products, to identify new global opportunities and to link specific technologies with new products and markets". The typical skills possessed by these individuals would be in the areas of "specialised problem-solving" (e.g., research, product design), "problem-identifying" (e.g., marketing, customer communications) and "brokerage services" (e.g., financing); see Levi-Faur (1997: 365) for a discussion.

type (assuming these skills are not possible for AI algorithms to replicate). Guessing future new job roles would be problematic even at the best of times, as the technological changes driving them could depend upon the coming together of as yet unrelated complementary technologies – as has so often been the case with recent transformative innovations (e.g., biotechnology, ICT).

As such, we are left with the contentious (some might say uncomfortable) notion that the gig economy represents a transition from a "wage" economy to a future where the human element is desired to be taken out of production altogether by firms seeking to cut costs and increase control, with all the attendant implications ("no economy?") of mass unemployment and a lumpen precariat class for widespread civil unrest and the growth of right-wing extremism (Standing 2012; 2017). Or are these concerns overstated? After all, there is a somewhat obvious point that goods and services produced by automated systems are intended with consumption by humans in mind. That is, issues of automation and consumption are still very much grounded in the traditional economic concept of aggregate demand; and moreover, effective demand. The implication here being, of course, that society would have to have sufficient incomes to maintain an effective level of consumption and that political means could be used to achieve this.

Concerns about how worker incomes will be derived from a reduced input to automated production and services processes amidst the increasing capture of physical, intellectual and financial capital by a small elite have led some (e.g., Standing 2017) to call for replacing wages with a "universal basic income" (UBI) that is independent of one's employment status, in order to provide basic economic security.

To date, such proposals have attracted considerable criticism (see Rees & Lansley 2016). Some suggest that a UBI is a blunt distributive mechanism, in that rich individuals would also receive it as well as poor and hence it makes no allowances for wealth. Similarly, a flat-rate UBI would make no allowances for additional circumstances such as having dependents (e.g., children). As such, a UBI would move away from the concept of welfare payments as being benefits secured by social security contributions in one's lifetime to that of income as a *right*. Others simply suggest that the "public" would not welcome the notion of people being paid, irrespective of whether they chose to work (*ibid.*). Responding to these criticisms (and the notion that a UBI could be used as a pretext to reduce public services), Rees and

Lansley argue that: "A UBI scheme should be seen as a supplement to wider provision of public services, and not as a substitute. A continuing and strong role for the public provision of key public services and other forms of state intervention including a generous living wage remains essential" (*ibid.*: 12).

However, Rubery (2019), writing from a gender perspective, argues that a UBI could have deleterious effects on women's labour market participation, as it could further entrench their status as care providers if formerly unpaid domestic work comes under its auspices. This is a valid criticism in that gender segregation could be aggravated until "social norms change so that everyone is expected to be a care giver as well as a breadwinner, the risks of such policies would be the withdrawal of female labor …" (2019: 101). The implication is clear here that policies to support a UBI should be cognizant of the gendered division of labour and should not come at the expense of female participation in waged work.

The technological changes associated with the 4IR have generated concerns over gender equality in terms of work. Some fear that a reduced volume of work could prompt a return to calls for women to have a reduced labour force participation, or that increased intermittency of work could threaten the foundations of rights such as maternity leave (see Rubery 2019). However, as Rubery (2019: 91) argues: "changes in gender relations may not only rule out a return to domestic work in the face of job shortage but may also be shaping access to newly-created jobs in ways that are not easily predictable. It is women who have taken the majority of higher-skilled jobs over recent years …". Indeed, OECD data (cited in Rubery 2019: 95) suggested that women comprised 8 million of the 12 million higher-skilled jobs generated in the European Union between 2003 and 2015. In addition, for Rubery, the fact that women on average have lower wages might reduce pressures to automate and thereby displace female workers, particularly in those sectors reinforcing the gender stereotype of requiring strong interpersonal skills or otherwise an emotional labour element (*ibid.*: 94).

The growth of the gig economy has also had implications for the nature of labour market participation and work–life balance over one's life-cycle. In part this is linked to wider structural issues in the economy that pertain to inter-generational inequality, most pertinently, in terms of the housing market. Home ownership rates in the UK continue to decline, with the growth of the private rental market particularly noticeable since 2007 (DWP 2019), as shown in Figure 5.1 below. Indeed, at the younger end of the spectrum,

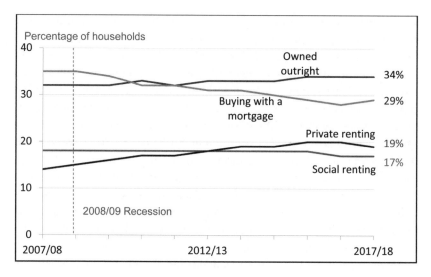

Figure 5.1 UK Households by tenure, 2007/08–2017/18

Source: Family Resources Survey 2017/18 (DWP 2019)

home ownership in many countries is becoming increasingly out of reach. In the UK the average price of a house (£283,000 in 2018) stood at 7.73 times that of the mean full-time employee wage (which was £36,611 in the same period), having increased from 4.34 times that of the mean full-time employee wage in 1999 (ONS 2019a; 2019b).

In this context, it should not be surprising that the number of "young adults" (i.e., those aged 20–34) living with their parents in the UK has increased from one in five in 2008 to one in four in 2015 (ONS 2016). For those not living with their parents, renting overtook home ownership for those aged 25–29 during 2004, and for those aged 30–34 during 2011 (*ibid.*). The gig economy, with its fluid nature and volatile earnings, is antithetical to the construct of taking out a mortgage with the fixed nominal debt repayment commitments over a number of years that this entails. To the extent that such forms of work become more extant, then the difficulties faced by younger workers trying to scale the property ladder will only become more acute.

At the older end of the spectrum, it is undoubtedly true that working in the gig economy might provide older workers, or retirees in particular, with a flexible means to stay connected in the labour market if full-time or regular working no longer appeals to them. For those who receive a pension the opportunity to combine this with supplementary paid work could have extra appeal. Indeed, a majority of pension schemes allow for some modicum of part-time work, even with one's previous employer where the company pension was accrued. However, the erosion in state pension entitlements across countries (Duvvury *et al.* 2018) and raising of the retirement age (AgeUK 2019; European Commission 2019; Oxlade 2017), could mean that for some older workers, participation in the gig economy is not through choice, but via necessity, in order to combat diminished earnings later in life. Structural change and plant closure could also affect older workers particularly in this regard, having to shift from formerly secure jobs into a labour market where the pressure will be on them to take whatever "job" may be on offer (Bailey & De Ruyter 2015).

However, as seen, there are signs that trade unions and government are waking up to the potential problems and long-term threats that the lack of regulation in the gig economy will have for society. As noted in the previous chapter, in December 2018, the UK government announced its Good Work Plan, arising from the Taylor Report, to overhaul workers' rights for the twenty-first century. While not offering radical change in terms of outlawing zero-hours contracts or introducing stringent labour requirements for gig employers (as per calls from the TUC), the plan is potentially a first step in regulating the emerging working environment and it recognizes the future potential growth of the gig economy. In contrast, the German government appears to place a stronger emphasis on worker participation in addressing the challenges posed by the 4IR, with the establishment of a tripartite framework (the "Digital Workplace platform") under the Ministry of Labour, which is overseen by the requisite minister and the Chairman of *IG Metall*, a large union conglomerate (Schroeder 2016: 8).

The consequences of automation may force a re-evaluation by society of the current focus on the commodification of work represented by the gig economy. Rubery captures many of these issues poignantly when she states that:

> [p]erhaps the only upside of the predicted disruption to labor markets materializes is that it should provide an opportunity to rethink how work and labor markets are organized and enable a

move towards more gender-equal sharing of wage work and unpaid care work, accommodated by an overdue trend toward shorter, not longer, full-time hours and more rights to combine care and work. *Whether or not that opportunity will be taken depends upon political will and not on the technology itself* (2019: 91, our emphasis).

As such, the gig economy could be seen as a (necessary) step towards more work–life balance, gender equality and concern for community and environmental sustainability as opposed to a narrow concern on profit. Rather than solely interpret the emergence of the gig economy in negative terms, it could be used to re-evaluate the nature of work and the position of work in terms of one's life trajectory. With the extension in lifespans and delayed entry into marriage and family for young people entering the world of work today, concepts such as childhood, adolescence and adulthood, with the responsibilities it carries have all experienced change – as evidenced by the emergence of terms such as "kidult" or "adultescent". These terms are not just marketing clichés but point to conscious decisions by individuals to delay the conventional trappings of adulthood and engage in "child-like" pursuits, and for which the world of work is adjusting to. Gaming (computer games, table games, etc.), for example, has traditionally been seen as a "childish" activity. However, it is not only tolerated but actively encouraged by tech firms, for example, which see it as a means to reduce stress and foster team spirit and creativity.

Of course, the attendant dangers of work intensification and the erosion of the boundary between work and leisure that the technology underpinning the gig economy has engendered remain ever-present. Glamorous notions of being footloose without the trappings of family dependents, as depicted in the communal work-living spaces espoused by companies such as WeWork/WeLive, have been described as preserving a lifestyle – at best – akin to maintaining a university student experience well into one's 30s (Harris 2018). As such, this needs to be weighed up against the nature of "home", "family" and "community" that some commentators (*ibid.*) argue such arrangements lack. Indeed, as mirrored in the UK housing market data presented above, for many, such patterns of working and living might not be by choice, but rather necessity in a fluid, atomised labour market.

Considering the nature of gig work in its wider (precarious work) sense that we have explored in this book, the contingency of labour market participation by those in highly precarious forms of work only further reiterates the need for ensuring that work "pays". Moreover, there is a clear imperative to ensure that "work" is posited in a wider system of regulation and benefits that aid personal and professional development.

However, we would argue that the future is ours to shape – hence, the opposite scenarios of technological utopia or dystopia are entirely possible. The key point is that as technology has evolved to date, so have regulatory frameworks designed to limit the negative consequences of the new systems of production unleashed thereof. The danger comes from any growing disenchantment and disengagement from the political process that would otherwise act to limit the power of "big tech" (government or private corporation). The opportunity is that technology is finally reaching a stage whereby it is possible to realize a society where a basic decent standard of living is possible for all across the globe and that humanity should live without the need for, in George Orwell's phrase, "brute labour". However, it remains to be seen where developments in the gig economy take us.

References

AgeUK 2019. "Changes to State Pension age". Available at: https://www.ageuk.org.uk/ information-advice/money-legal/pensions/state-pension/changes-to-state-pension-age/ (accessed 2 April 2019).

Ainge-Roy, H. 2016. "Zero-hour contracts banned in New Zealand". *The Guardian*, 11 March. Available at: https://www.theguardian.com/world/2016/mar/11/zero-hour-contracts-banned-in-new-zealand (accessed 22 July 2018).

Albert, S. & K. Bradley 1998. "Professional temporary agencies, women and professional discretion: implications for organization and management". *British Journal of Management* 9: 261–72.

Allan, C., M. O'Donnell & D. Peetz 1999. "Three dimensions of labour utilisation: job broadening, employment insecurity and work intensification". In *Proceedings of the 13th AIRAANZ Conference*, 4–6 February, Adelaide, Australia; Track 1: Refereed Papers.

Aloisi, A. 2016. "Commoditized workers: case study research on labor law issues arising from a set of 'on-demand/gig economy' platforms". *Comparative Labor Law & Policy Journal* 37(3): 653–90. Available at: http://dx.doi.org/10.2139/ssrn.2637485 (accessed 27 July 2018).

Atkinson, J. 1984. "Manpower strategies for flexible organisations". *Personnel Management*, August: 28–31.

Atkinson, J. 1987. "Flexibility or fragmentation: the United Kingdom labour market in the eighties". *Labour and Society* 12(1): 87–105.

Australian Bureau of Statistics (ABS) 2017. "Catalogue 6333.0 – *Characteristics of Employment*", August 2017. Available at: http://www.abs.gov.au/AUSSTATS/abs@.nsf/Details Page/6333.0August%202017?OpenDocument (accessed 27 May 2018).

Bailey, D. & A. De Ruyter 2015. "Plant closures, precariousness and policy responses: revisiting the MG Rover case". *Policy Studies* 36(4): 363–83.

Barsky, J. & C. Coloma 2017. *Deep Undercover: My Secret life and Tangled Allegiances as a KGB Spy in America*. Carol Stream, IL: Tyndale House.

Becker, G. 1964. *Human Capital Theory*. New York: Columbia University Press.

Birch, A. 1998. *The British System of Government*. London: Routledge.

Bosch, G. 2004. "Towards a new standard employment relationship in western Europe". *British Journal of Industrial Relations* 42(4): 617–36.

Braverman, H. 1974. *Labor and Monopoly Capital: The Degradation of Work in the Twentieth Century*. New York: Monthly Review Press.

Brinkley, I. 2013. "*Flexibility or insecurity? Exploring the rise in zero hours contracts*" (August). The Work Foundation, Lancaster University. Available at: https://csgconsult.com/wp-content/uploads/2014/03/339_flexibility-or-insecurity-final.pdf (accessed 9 February 2018).

Brooks, B. 1985. "Aspects of casual and part-time employment". *Journal of Industrial Relations* 27(2): 158–71.

Brosnan, P. 1996. "Labour markets and social deprivation". *Labour and Industry* 7(2): 3–31.

Brosnan, P., J. Burgess & D. Rea 1992. "Two ways to skin a cat: government policy and labour market reform in Australia and New Zealand". *International Contributions to Labour Studies* 2: 17–44.

Brown, A. *et al.* 2007. "Job quality and the economics of new labour: a critical appraisal using subjective survey data". *Cambridge Journal of Economics* 31: 941–71.

Brown, M. 2010. "Work in a spiritual place: an ethnographic study of the nature of organisational life in self-sustaining spiritual communities". Working paper, Birmingham City Business School.

Bureau of Labor Statistics (BLS) 2018a. "Electronically mediated employment". Available at: https://www.bls.gov/cps/electronically-mediated-employment.htm (accessed 4 October 2018).

Bureau of Labor Statistics (BLS) 2018b. "Contingent and alternative employment arrangements summary". Available at: https://www.bls.gov/news.release/conemp.nr0.htm (accessed 4 October 2018).

Burgess, J. 1997. "The flexible firm and the growth of non-standard employment". *Labour and Industry* 7(3): 83–102.

Burgess, J. 1995. "Does non-standard employment growth confirm the model of the flexible firm?" University of Newcastle, Australia: Employment Studies Centre, Research Paper 21.

Cain, R. 2016. "Responsibilising recovery: lone and low-paid parents, universal credit and the gendered contradictions of UK welfare reform". *British Politics* 11(4): 488–507.

Caire, G. 1989. "Atypical wage employment in France". In G. Rodgers & J. Rodgers (eds), *Precarious Jobs in Labour Market Regulation: The Growth of Atypical Employment in Western Europe*, 75–108. Geneva: International Labour Organization.

Campbell, I. 1993. "Labour market flexibility in Australia: enhancing management prerogative?". *Labour and Industry* 5(3): 1–32.

Campbell, I. & R. Price 2016. "Precarious work and precarious workers: towards an improved conceptualisation". *Economic and Labour Relations Review* 27(3): 314–32.

Cappelli, P. 2008. "Talent management for the Twenty-First century". *Harvard Business Review*, March: 1–9.

Cappelli, P. 1995. "Rethinking employment". *British Journal of Industrial Relations* 33(4): 563–602.

Cappelli, P. & J. Keller 2014. "Talent management: conceptual approaches and practical challenges". *Annual Review of Organizational Psychology and Organizational Behavior* 1: 305–31.

Casey, B. 2004. "The OECD jobs strategy and the European employment strategy: two views of the labour market and the welfare state." *European Journal of Industrial Relations* 10(3): 329–52.

Chapman, A. 2006. "Unfair dismissal law and work choices: from safety net standard to legal privilege". *Economic and Labour Relations Review* 16(2): 237–64.

Cherry, M. & A. Aloisi 2018. "A critical examination of a third employment category for on-demand work: in comparative perspective". In N. Davidson, M. Finck & J. Infranca (eds), *Cambridge Handbook on the Law of the Sharing Economy*, 316–27. Cambridge: Cambridge University Press.

Chou, S.-Y. 2019. "The Fourth Industrial Revolution: digital fusion with Internet of Things". *Columbia Journal of International Affairs* 72(1): 107–20.

Coase, R. 1937. "The nature of the firm". *Economica* 4(16): 386–405.

Collman, A. 2014. "Google employees reveal life is so sweet they LIVED at work rent-free thanks to the tech giant"s awesome perks". *Mail Online*, 10 September. Available at: http://www.dailymail.co.uk/news/article-2750652/Former-Google-employees-brag-long-lived-work-rent-free-thanks-tech-giant-s-awesome-perks.html (accessed 21 July 2018).

Commons, J. 1931. "Institutional economics". *American Economic Review* 21: 648–57.

Coyle-Shapiro, J. & I. Kessler 2000. "Consequences of the psychological contract for the employment relationship: a large scale survey". *Journal of Management Studies* 37(7): 903–30.

Davidov, G. 2004. "Joint employer status in triangular employment relationships". *British Journal of Industrial Relations* 42(4): 727–46.

De Ruyter, A. & J. Burgess 2003. "Growing labour insecurity in Australia and the UK in the midst of jobs growth: beware the Anglo-Saxon model!". *European Journal of Industrial Relations* 9(2): 223–43.

De Ruyter, A. *et al.* 2008. "Agency working and the degradation of public service employment: the case of nurses and social workers". *International Journal of Human Resource Management* 19(3): 432–45.

De Ruyter, A. *et al.* 2011. "Labor standards, gender and decent work in newly industrialized countries: promoting the good society". In J. Marangos (ed.) *Alternative Perspectives on the Good Society*, 121–46. Basingstoke: Palgrave Macmillan

De Stefano, V. 2016. "The rise of the 'just-in-time workforce': on-demand work, crowd-work and labour protection in the 'gig-economy'". Conditions of Work and Employment Series Report no. 71. Geneva: International Labour Organization.

Deery, S. & A. Mahony 1994. "Temporal flexibility: management strategies and employee preferences in the retail industry". *Journal of Industrial Relations* 36(3): 332–52.

Department for Work & Pensions (DWP) UK 2019. *Family Resources Survey 2017/18*. Available at: https://assets.publishing.service.gov.uk/government/uploads/system/uploads/attachment_data/file/791271/family-resources-survey-2017-18.pdf (accessed 1 April 2019).

Doeringer, P. & M. Piore 1971. *Internal Labour Markets and Manpower Analysis*. Lexington, MA: Heath.

Drahokoupil, J. & A. Piasna 2017. "Work in the platform economy: beyond lower transaction costs". *Intereconomics* 52(6): 335–40.

Duvvury, N., Á. Ní Léime & A. Callan 2018. "Erosion of pension rights: experiences of older women in Ireland". *European Journal of Cultural and Political Sociology* 5(3): 266–94.

European Commission 2019. *Germany: Pensions and other old age benefits*. Available at: https://ec.europa.eu/social/main.jsp?catId=1111&intPageId=4554&langId=en (accessed 2 April 2019).

EurWORK 2016. "Representativeness of the European social partner organisations: temporary agency work sector". European Foundation for the Improvement of Living and Working Conditions. Available at: https://www.eurofound.europa.eu/observatories/eurwork/comparative-information/representativeness-of-the-european-social-partner-org anisations-temporary-agency-work-sector (accessed 17 April 2018).

Evening Standard 2018. "London taxi protest: black cab drivers stage demo against TfL and Uber", 15 January.

Ewing, K. 2014. "Regulating for decent work and the effectiveness of labour law". *New Zealand Journal of Employment Relations* 39(2): 3–21.

Fleming, P. 2017. "The human capital hoax: work, debt and insecurity in the era of Uberization". *Organization Studies* 38(5): 691–709.

Frey, C. & M. Osborne 2013. "The future of employment: how susceptible are jobs to computerisation". Oxford Martin Programme on the Impacts of Future Technology. Available at: http://enliza.es/SECCIONES_1/1_EL%20FUTURO%20DEL%20TRABAJO/RECURSOS/The_Future_of_Employment_OMS_Working_Paper.pdf (accessed 27 July 2018).

Friedman, G. 2014a. "The rise of the gig economy". Dollars & Sense: Real World Economics. Available at: http://www.dollarsandsense.org/archives/2014/0314friedman.html (accessed 23 April 2018).

Friedman, G. 2014b. "Workers without employers: shadow corporations and the rise of the gig economy". *Review of Keynesian Economics* 2(2): 171–88.

Friedman, M. 1979. *Free to Choose: A Personal Statement*. London: Pelican.

Gerfin, M., M. Lechner & H. Steiger 2005. "Does subsidised temporary employment get the unemployed back to work? An econometric analysis of two different schemes". *Labour Economics* 12(6): 807–35.

Gharibi, M., R. Boutaba & S. Waslander 2016. "Internet of drones", *IEEE Access* 4: 1148–62. Available at: https://ieeexplore.ieee.org/stamp/stamp.jsp?arnumber=7423671 (accessed 18 March 2019).

Goodall, W. *et al.* 2017. "The rise of mobility as a service: reshaping how urbanites get around". *Deloitte Review* 20: 113–29. Available at: https://wellryde.com/wp-content/uploads/2018/03/deloitte-nl-cb-ths-rise-of-mobility-as-a-service.compressed.pdf (accessed 29 July 2018).

Graham, M., I. Hjorth & V. Lehdonvirta 2017. "Digital labour and development: impacts of global digital labour platforms and the gig economy on worker livelihoods". *Transfer: European Review of Labour and Research* 23(2): 135–62.

Grimshaw, D. & J. Rubery 1998. "Integrating the internal and external labour markets". *Cambridge Journal of Economics* 22(2): 199–220.

Grimshaw, D., J. Earnshaw & G. Hebson 2003. "Private sector provision of supply teachers: a case of legal swings and professional roundabouts". *Journal of Education Policy* 18(3): 267–88.

Guardian Australia 2018. "Uber drivers log off in Australia-wide protest against low fares", 5 August.

Hall, P. & D. Soskice 2001. "An introduction to varieties of capitalism". In P. Hall & D. Soskice (eds), *Varieties of Capitalism: The Institutional Foundations of Comparative Advantage*, 1–69. New York: Oxford University Press.

Harris, J. 2018. "In a world of digital nomads, we will all be made homeless". *The Guardian*, 18 June. Available at: https://www.theguardian.com/commentisfree/2018/jun/18/digital-nomad-homeless-tech-work (accessed 4 July 2018).

Harvey, C. & S. Kanwal 2000. "Self employed IT knowledge workers and the experience of flexibility: evidence from the United Kingdom". In K. Purcell (ed.), *Changing Boundaries in Employment*, 104–32. Bristol: Bristol Academic Press.

Harvey, G. *et al.* 2017. "Neo-villeiny and the service sector: the case of hyper flexible and precarious work in fitness centres". *Work, Employment & Society* 31(1): 19–35.

Helbing, D., *et al.* 2017. "Will democracy survive big data and artificial intelligence?". Available at: https://www.bsfrey.ch/articles/D_283_2017.pdf (accessed 4 June 2018).

Hobbes, T. 2008. *Leviathan*. M. Missner (ed.). London: Routledge.

Hofstede, G. 2001. *Cultures Consequences: Comparing Values, Behaviours, Institutions, and Organisations Across Nations*. Second edition. Thousand Oaks, CA: Sage.

Hyman, R. 1987. "Strategy or structure? Capital, labour and control". *Work, Employment and Society* 1(1): 25–55.

ILO 1994. *The Role of Private Employment Agencies in the Functioning of Labour Markets.* Geneva: International Labour Organization.

ILO 2016. *Non-Standard Employment Around the World: Understanding Challenges, Shaping Prospects.* Geneva: International Labour Organization.

ILO 2018. "Trade union density rate and collective bargaining coverage rate". Available at: http://www.ilo.org/ilostat/faces/oracle/webcenter/portalapp/pagehierarchy/Page3.jspx? (accessed 18 October 2018).

ILO 2018a. "Temporary employees by sex". Available at: http://www.ilo.org/ilostat/faces/oracle/webcenter/portalapp/pagehierarchy/Page27.jspx? (accessed 9 February 2018).

ILO 2018b. "Employment distribution by status in employment". Available at: http://www.ilo.org/ilostat/faces/oracle/webcenter/portalapp/pagehierarchy/Page27.jspx? (accessed 9 February 2018).

Jaehrling, K. & P. Méhout 2012. "Varieties of institutional avoidance: employers' strategies in low-waged service sector occupations in France and Germany". *Socio-Economic Review* (advance online access), 1–24. Available at: https://www.researchgate.net/profile/Philippe_Mehaut/publication/260277647_%27Varieties_of_institutional_avoidance%27_Employers%27_strategies_in_low-waged_service_sector_occupations_in_France_and_Germany/links/574d8dcb08ae061b33033601/Varieties-of-institutional-avoidance-Employers-strategies-in-low-waged-service-sector-occupations-in-France-and-Germany.pdf (accessed 24 May 2018).

Kelliher, C. & D. Anderson 2010. "Doing more with less? Flexible working practices and the intensification of work". *Human Relations* 63(1): 83–106.

Kenney, M. & J. Zysman 2016. "The rise of the platform economy". *Issues in Science and Technology*, spring edn: 61–9.

Kerr, C. 1954. *Balkanization of Labor Markets.* Berkeley, CA: University of California.

Kirkpatrick, I. *et al.* 2011. "'Practising what they preach?' The disconnect between the state as user and the state as regulator of employment agencies". *International Journal of Human Resource Management* 22(18): 3711–26.

Kunda, G., S. Barley & J. Evans 2002. "Why do contractors contract? The experience of highly skilled technical professionals in a contingent labour market". *Industrial and Labor Relations Review* 55(2): 234–61.

Kuhn, K. 2016. "The rise of the 'gig economy' and implications for understanding work and workers". *Industrial and Organizational Psychology* 9(1): 157–62.

Lang, C., I. Schömann & S. Clauwaert 2013. "Atypical forms of employment contracts in times of crisis". European Trade Union Institute working paper 2013.03. Available at: https://papers.ssrn.com/sol3/papers.cfm?abstract_id=2336982 (accessed 5 July 2018).

Ledwith, S. 2012. "Gender politics in trade unions: the representation of women between exclusion and inclusion". *Transfer: European Review of Labour and Research* 18(2): 185–99.

Lehdonvirta, V. 2018. "Flexibility in the gig economy: managing time on three online piecework platforms". *New Technology, Work and Employment* 33(1): 13–29.

Lepak, D. & S. Snell 1999. "The human resource architecture: towards a theory of human capital allocation and development". *Academy of Management Review* 24(1): 31–48.

Levi-Faur, D. 1997. "Economic nationalism: from Friedrich List to Robert Reich". *Review of International Studies* 23: 359–70.

Lewis, P., A. Thornhill & M. Saunders 2003. *Employee Relations: Understanding the Employment Relationship.* Harlow: Pearson.

Machin, S. 1997. "The decline of labour market institutions and the rise in wage inequality in Britain". *European Economic Review* 41(3–5): 647–57.

Marsden, D. 1986. *The End of Economic Man*. New York: St Martin's Press.

Marx, K. [1887] 2018. *Capital: Volume 1*. Champaign, IL: Modern Barbarian Press.

McCann, D. 2007. *Regulating Flexible Work*. Oxford: Oxford University Press.

McNabb, R. & K. Whitfield 1998. "Testing for segmentation: an establishment-level analysis". *Cambridge Journal of Economics* 22(3): 347–65.

Miller, J. 2015. "The labor prospect: is there an on-demandate?". *The American Prospect*, 15 December. Available at: http://prospect.org/article/labor-prospect-there-demandate (accessed 20 May 2018).

Monaghan, A. 2017. "Record 910,000 UK workers on zero-hours contracts". *The Guardian*, 3 March. Available at: https://www.theguardian.com/business/2017/mar/03/zero-hours-contracts-uk-record-high (accessed 14 July 2018).

Moyer-Lee, J. 2018. "When will 'gig economy' companies admit that their workers have rights?". *The Guardian*, 14 June. Available at: https://www.theguardian.com/commentisfree/2018/jun/14/gig-economy-workers-pimlico-plumbers-employment-rights (accessed 10 July 2018).

Norris, K. 1983. *The Economics of Australian Labour Markets*. Melbourne: Longman Cheshire.

Nübler, I. 2016. "New technologies: a jobless future or a golden age of job creation?". ILO Research Department working paper No. 13. Available at: https://www.researchgate.net/profile/Irmgard_Nuebler/publication/315408966_New_technologies_A_jobless_future_or_a_golden_age_of_job_creation/links/58cfc56ba6fdccff68e2e369/New-technologies-A-jobless-future-or-a-golden-age-of-job-creation.pdf (accessed 26 July 2018).

Office for National Statistics (ONS) 2016. "Why are more young people living with their parents?". Available at: https://www.ons.gov.uk/peoplepopulationandcommunity/births deathsandmarriages/families/articles/whyaremoreyoungpeoplelivingwiththeir parents/2016-02-22 (accessed 1 April 2019).

Office for National Statistics (ONS) 2018. "Trends in self-employment in the UK". Available at: https://www.ons.gov.uk/employmentandlabourmarket/peopleinwork/employmentand employeetypes/articles/trendsinselfemploymentintheuk/2018-02-07 (accessed 4 June 2018).

Office for National Statistics (ONS) 2019a. "UK house price index". Available at: https://www.ons. gov.uk/economy/inflationandpriceindices/datasets/housepriceindexannualtables2039 (accessed 1 April 2019).

Office for National Statistics (ONS) 2019b. "Annual survey of hours and earnings (ASHE)". Available at: https://www.ons.gov.uk/employmentandlabourmarket/peopleinwork/ earningsandworkinghours/datasets/workbasedtraveltoworkareaashetable11 (accessed 1 April 2019).

Oxlade, A. 2017. "World pension ages on the rise: when will you retire?" Available at: https:// www.schroders.com/en/insights/economics/world-pension-ages-on-the-rise-when-will-you-retire/ (accessed 2 April 2019).

Philbeck, T. & N. Davis 2019. "The Fourth Industrial Revolution: shaping a new era". *Columbia Journal of International Affairs* 72(1): 17–22.

Piketty, T. 2016. "We must rethink globalization, or Trumpism will prevail". *The Guardian*, 16 November. Available at: https://www.theguardian.com/commentisfree/2016/nov/16/ globalization-trump-inequality-thomas-piketty (accessed 24 July 2018).

Pink, D. 2001. *Free Agent Nation: How America's New Independent Workers Are Transforming the Way We Live*. New York: Warner.

Porter, M. 1985. *Competitive Advantage: Creating and Sustaining Superior Performance*. New York: The Free Press.

Preston, A. 1997. "Where are we now with human capital theory?". *Economic Record* 73(220): 51–78.

Purcell, J., K. Purcell & S. Tailby 2004. "Temporary work agencies: here today, gone tomorrow?". *British Journal of Industrial Relations* 42(4): 705–25.

Raveaud, G. 2007. "The European employment strategy: towards more and better jobs?". *Journal of Common Market Studies* 45(2): 411–34.

Rees, H. & S. Lansley 2016. "Universal Basic Income: an idea whose time has come?" *Compass*. Available at: https://www.ezyloada.com/wp-content/uploads/2016/05/UniversalBasic IncomeByCompass-Spreads.pdf (accessed 18 March 2019).

Reich, R. 1991. *The Work of Nations: Preparing Ourselves for Twenty-First Century Capitalism*. Hemel Hempstead: Simon & Shuster.

Reuters News 2018. "Taxi drivers protest against Uber 'invasion' in Greece", 6 March. Available at: https://www.reuters.com/...protests...uber/taxi-drivers-protest-against-uber-invasion-in-gr... (accessed 2 April 2019).

Ritzer, G. 1993. *The McDonaldization of Society*. Newbury Park, CA: Pine Forge Press.

Rouse, M. 2019. "Drone (unmanned aerial vehicle, UAV)". *IoT Agenda*. Available at: https:// internetofthingsagenda.techtarget.com/definition/drone (accessed 11 March 2019).

Rousseau, D. 1995. *Psychological Contracts in Organizations: Understanding Written and Unwritten Agreements*. London: Sage.

Rubery, J. 1978. "Structured labour markets, worker organisation and low pay". *Cambridge Journal of Economics* 2(1): 17–36.

Rubery, J. 2019. "A gender lens on the future of work". *Columbia Journal of International Affairs* 72(1): 91–105.

Rubery, J. & D. Grimshaw 2015. "Precarious work and the commodification of the employment relationship: the case of zero hours in the UK and mini jobs in Germany". In G. Bäcker, S. Lehndorff & C. Weinkopf (eds), *Den Arbeitsmarkt verstehen, um ihn zu gestalten*, 239–54. Wiesbaden: Springer.

Salh, S., M. Nyfoudi & A. De Ruyter 2017. "Future regulation of the UK workforce". In D. Bailey & L. Budd (eds), *The Political Economy of Brexit*, 63–79. Newcastle upon Tyne: Agenda.

Schroeder, W. 2016. "Germany's Industry 4.0 strategy: Rhine capitalism in the age of digitalisation". Available at: https://www.uni-kassel.de/fb05/fileadmin/datas/fb05/FG_Politik wissenschaften/PSBRD/FES-London_Schroeder_Germanys_Industrie_4.0_Strategy.pdf (accessed 15 March 2019).

Sengenberger, W. 1981. "Labour market segmentation and the business cycle". In F. Wilkinson (ed.), *The Dynamics of Labour Market Segmentation*, 243–60. London: Academic Press.

Siebert, H. 1997. "Labor market rigidities: at the root of unemployment in Europe". *Journal of Economic Perspectives* 11(3): 37–54.

Simms, M. 2010. "Trade union responses to precarious work". Industrial Relations Research Unit, University of Warwick. Available at: http://archive.uva-aias.net/uploaded_files/ regular/BARSORIReportUK.pdf (accessed 3 August 2018).

Simon, H. 1997. *Models of Bounded Rationality, Vol. 3: Empirically Grounded Economic Reason*. Cambridge, MA: MIT Press.

Simon, J.-P. 2016. "How to catch a unicorn: an exploration of the universe of tech companies with high market capitalisation". Joint Research Centre working paper JRC100719 (Seville site).

Smith, A. 1970. *The Wealth of Nations*. A. Skinner (ed.). Harmondsworth: Penguin.

Standing, G. 1997. "Globalization, labour flexibility and insecurity: the era of market regulation". *European Journal of Industrial Relations* 3(1): 7–37.

Standing, G. 2012. "The precariat: why it needs deliberative democracy". Open Democracy. Available at: https://www.opendemocracy.net/guy-standing/precariat-why-it-needs-deliberative-democracy (accessed 28 July 2018).

Standing, G. 2017. *Basic Income: And How We Can Make It Happen*. Gretna, LA: Pelican.

Stanford, J. 2017. "The resurgence of gig work: historical and theoretical perspectives". *Economic and Labour Relations Review* 28(3): 382–401.

Stewart, A. & J. Stanford 2017. "Regulating work in the gig economy: what are the options?" *Economic and Labour Relations Review* 28(3): 420–37.

Supreme Court of the UK 2014. *Judgment: Clyde and Co LLP and Another (Respondents) v Bates van Winkelhof (Appelant)*. Available at: https://www.supremecourt.uk/decided-cases/docs/UKSC_2012_0229_Judgment.pdf (accessed 30 July 2018).

Taylor, N. 2018. "The Republic of Ireland and Northern Ireland: technology enablement for a frictionless smart border". Centre for Brexit Studies working paper. Available at: https://www.bcu.ac.uk/centre-for-brexit-studies/reports/working-papers (accessed 11 March 2019).

Technopedia 2019a. "Definition: artificial intelligence (AI)". Available at https://www.techopedia.com/definition/190/artificial-intelligence-ai (accessed 13 March 2019).

Technopedia 2019b. "Definition: weak AI". Available at: https://www.techopedia.com/definition/31621/weak-artificial-intelligence-weak-ai (accessed 13 March 2019).

Technopedia 2019c. "Definition: strong AI". Available at: https://www.techopedia.com/definition/31622/strong-artificial-intelligence-strong-ai (accessed 13 March 2019).

Technopedia 2019d. "Definition: machine learning". Available at: https://www.techopedia.com/definition/8181/machine-learning (accessed 13 March 2019).

Thompson, E. 1963. *The Making of the English Working Class*. London: Victor Gollancz.

Thörnquist, A. 2015. "False self-employment and other precarious forms of employment in the 'grey area' of the labour market". *International Journal of Comparative Labour Law and Industrial Relations* 31(4): 411–29.

Thurow, L. 1996. *The Future of Capitalism*. Sydney: Allen & Unwin.

UK Parliament 2018. *A Framework for Modern Employment*. Available at: https://publications.parliament.uk/pa/cm201719/cmselect/cmworpen/352/35206.htm#_idTextAnchor026 (accessed 28 July 2018).

Wilkinson, F. & M. White 1994. "Product market pressures and employer responses". In J. Rubery & F. Wilkinson (eds), *Employer Strategy and the Labour Market*, 111–37. New York: Oxford University Press.

Williams, S. & P. Scott 2010. "Shooting the past? The modernisation of Conservative Party employment relations policy under David Cameron". *Industrial Relations Journal* 41(1): 4–18.

Williamson, O. 1985. *The Economic Institutions of Capitalism: Firms, Markets, Relational Contracting*. New York: The Free Press.

World Employment Confederation (WEC) 2017. "Economic report: enabling work, adaptation, security & prosperity". Available at: http://www.wecglobal.org/fileadmin/templates/ciett/docs/Economic_Report/WEC_Economic_report_2017_Final.pdf (accessed 21 May 2018).

Zervas, G., D. Proserpio & J. Byers 2017. "The rise of the sharing economy: estimating the impact of Airbnb on the hotel industry". *Journal of Marketing Research* 54(5): 687–705.

Index